GENTLEMEN FREEHOLDERS

The Institute of Early American History and Culture is sponsored jointly by the College of William and Mary and Colonial Williamsburg, Incorporated

GENTLEMEN FREEHOLDERS

Political Practices in Washington's Virginia

BY

CHARLES S. SYDNOR

Published for
THE INSTITUTE OF
EARLY AMERICAN HISTORY AND CULTURE
at Williamsburg, Virginia
by
THE UNIVERSITY OF NORTH CAROLINA PRESS
CHAPEL HILL

To My Sons
CHARLES SACKETT SYDNOR, *Jr.*
VICTOR BROWN SYDNOR

Acknowledgments

Of the many persons who have assisted in this study, and to all of whom I am grateful, there are three who have been notably helpful: my Wife, Mr. William W. Abbot, III, and Dr. Noble E. Cunningham, Jr. An award by the Library of Congress and grants by the Duke University Research Council speeded its completion. Finally, I wish to express my gratitude to Oxford University for permission to reprint some passages of my Inaugural Lecture as Harmsworth Professor of American History. This lecture was published at the Clarendon Press in 1951 under the title, *Political Leadership in Eighteenth-Century Virginia.*

C. S. S.

Duke University

Contents

GENTLEMEN FREEHOLDERS

CHAPTER ONE

Behind the Virginia Dynasty

IF WASHINGTON, Jefferson, Madison, and Marshall had never lived, the nation could not, of course, have benefited by their thoughts and actions; neither, for that matter, would it have received much profit from them, alive and in full possession of their powers, if they had been left in the obscurity of private life. Statesmen come to the helm of government only if society has ways of discovering men of extraordinary talent, character, and training and of elevating them, rather than their inferiors, to office. Democracy must do two things and do them well: it must develop men who are fit to govern, and it must select for office these men rather than their less worthy contemporaries.

To understand the making of any one of the leaders of revolutionary Virginia one should know much about the ancestry and family life, the education and friendships, and the host of other particular influences which made him the man that he was.[1] Biographers of Washington must write of his intimacy with the Fairfaxes and his work as a surveyor in the wilderness; Jefferson's biographers must tell of his friendship with George Wythe, learned student of law and of the classics, William Small, the ablest teacher in the College of

William and Mary, and Francis Fauquier, Governor of Virginia, child of the Enlightenment and man of the world. Those who write about Madison must consider his friendship with Jefferson; and the biographer of John Marshall must weigh the influence of his father, Thomas, and the impression made by a winter at Valley Forge when he saw patriots suffering because the government was too weak to supply them with food and clothing.

In ways such as these each of the leading men of revolutionary Virginia was influenced by innumerable circumstances peculiar to him alone that made him unlike any other person. But all of them were subjected to several general influences that gave a distinctive character to them as a group. With few exceptions, they were members of families that were well-to-do and that had enjoyed a favored place in society for several generations. If they had taken the trouble to look at old records, they would have found the names of their ancestors in lists of burgesses, councilors, justices, and vestrymen at the beginning of that century and before. The family traditions of the Randolphs, the Nelsons, the Pages, the Lees, the Harrisons, the Carters, the Byrds, and others were variant versions of Virginia history.

Neither the family's history nor the colony's history was always above reproach. The founders of these families sometimes used their political power to get lucrative public offices and extensive grants of land; in this way the economic foundation of many a great family was laid. But the attachment of these families to the social order and to the government that gave them prominence and prosperity was nonetheless strong. This attachment may be variously described as enlightened selfishness, family tradition, patriotism, or a sense of public responsibility; but whatever the dominant motive in the individual case, there existed in Virginia long before the American Revolution what Alexander Hamilton wanted to bring into existence in the nation: the firm attachment to government of the rich, the well-born, and the able.

The custom of filling offices with planters' sons made the homes of the gentry preliminary training schools for future officeholders. The social advantages enjoyed in these favored homes gave to their sons some preparation for entering the more sophisticated society of Williamsburg, Philadelphia, London, or Paris, should public service send them there. Inasmuch as the son was often following his father into public affairs, he could profit by his father's knowledge of public questions and important men. Because the father could afford it, the son was often given a superior education. At a time when American colleges were few and small, most of the Virginians who sat in the early Congresses and who served as governor in the first years of statehood were college men. A few had studied abroad, at the University of Edinburgh or at one of the Inns of Court, but most of them had attended an American institution. Princeton and especially William and Mary were the favorite colleges for Virginia youth.

Princeton, in this day of John Witherspoon, was the better college; but William and Mary, though small and poorly staffed, afforded an excellent extra-mural education in politics. Its location in the colonial capital gave to its students a remarkable opportunity to observe the operations of government. Those who were well connected could bring themselves to the attention of Richard Bland, Peyton Randolph, Robert Carter Nicholas, and the other powerful and experienced men who operated government. And those who cared for such things, as Jefferson did, could stand at the door of the House of Burgesses and hear the thrilling oratory of Patrick Henry. Few of the students equalled Jefferson in seizing the chance to learn from older men. But some of those who learned little from their professors or from the rulers of the province nevertheless learned the temperaments and character, the strength and weaknesses, of fellow students who would some day be fellow burgesses and fellow congressmen.[2]

In time the sons of planters became planters themselves and learned their first lessons in administration by managing their own farms or plantations. In some instances the establishment was small, but a visit today to Mount Vernon, Montpelier, Gunston Hall, and Monticello, or Carter's Grove and Shirley of the Carters, Westover of the Byrds, Stratford of the Lees, Brandon of the Harrisons, Bremo of the Cockes, Berry Hill of the Bruces, or the homes of other leading families of the eighteenth and early nineteenth centuries, leaves no doubt that many of these men were masters of large estates. Their broad acres and ample houses set the stage for independent and dignified living; but their lives were not carefree. The management of the economic, social, and political microcosm that was theirs was a heavy and multifarious responsibility. Plans had to be made and executed for maintaining buildings, for allocating fields to the several crops, for planting and harvesting, for providing food for man and beast, and for securing a money income by the sale of tobacco, wheat, and other commodities. There were unwilling laborers to be pushed on to their tasks, and problems as numerous and varied as the complexities of human nature to be settled among the slaves and within the master's immediate family.

Records had to be kept and letters written in longhand in

rooms without screened windows to keep out flies, mosquitoes, and moths. The planter knew the feel of plowed land under foot, the smell of manure, the heat of the sun, the bite of cold wind, the heavy breathing of an overworked horse, the holiday spirit of the quarters, and the sullen scowl of an angry slave. He learned to accommodate his plantation management to the inexorable laws of nature and his dealings with people to real men and women. Perhaps from these experiences he gained wisdom for public life. At any rate, in politics the Virginia planter seemed to understand that, although ideals and ultimate goals were worth striving for, legislation and political policy had to be fitted to Virginia and Virginians as they existed in the eighteenth century, to the nation as it was in 1789.

The planter, of course, could indulge in theories and speculations to his heart's content, and often did. He could experiment with unorthodox crops, methods of marketing, or ways of controlling human beings; but if his penchant for experimentation was too great or his judgment too frequently wrong, the error of his ways was made plainly and painfully obvious to him—and to his neighbors, for the planter's business operations were carried on in public. Untidy fields, scrawny livestock, and a dilapidated house gave notice through the countryside that the owner lacked energy, judgment, or some other quality essential to good management. A man who could not manage well his own affairs would hardly impress his neighbors as a man who ought to be entrusted with the management of public affairs. In eighteenth-century Virginia failure in business was seldom rewarded with a seat in the county court or in the legislature or with such offices as sheriff, clerk, or coroner.

The possession of power that was almost dictatorial over his own little world left its mark on the manners and character of the planter. With kindly humor, John Pendleton Kennedy described this effect:

"The solitary elevation of a country gentleman, well to do in the world, begets some magnificent notions. He becomes as infallible as the Pope; gradually acquires a habit of making long speeches; is apt to be impatient of contradiction, and is always very touchy on the point of honor. There is nothing more conclusive than a rich man's logic any where, but in the country, amongst his dependents, it flows with the smooth and unresisted course of a full stream irrigating a meadow, and depositing its mud in fertilizing luxuriance." [3]

Kennedy was by no means the only person to be impressed by the tendency of Virginia planters to be obstinate, haughty, opinionated, and headstrong.[4] But neither Kennedy nor anyone else observed in the planters such traits as obsequiousness, duplicity, or indecision. These qualities would have been unnatural and worse than useless in managing a plantation, controlling dependents, or dealing with neighboring farmers and planters. Nor were the manners and the habits of the planters a handicap in getting into office in eighteenth-century Virginia. It was fortunate for Jefferson, Washington, Marshall, Madison, and many of their colleagues, and for the nation as well, that they could win office without having to practice some of the arts and techniques that have proved useful in later times.

Planters, not lawyers, dominated the political scene in eighteenth-century Virginia. Although a good many men prominent in politics had been admitted to the bar, and some of them, like Marshall, made a career of their profession, there were more, like Jefferson, who were primarily planters. Others, like Mason and Madison, read law but were never admitted to the bar. Curious as it may seem, many of the county justices brought no knowledge of law to the bench though they naturally picked up some after becoming members of the county courts.

The practice of law before the county courts did bring one to the attention of the segment of society that chiefly possessed political power, and the lawyer therefore enjoyed an advantage in making a political career provided he was connected by family and other ties with the ruling class. But it was not the practice of law so much as the study of the history of law, especially constitutional history, and of political philosophy that distinguished this generation of Virginia statesmen. Jefferson reflected this emphasis in prescribing the course of studies for the Law School of the University of Virginia. Some of the great names of English constitutional history were perhaps better known in America than in England in the 1770's; a Virginia college founded in this decade was named for John Hampden and Algernon Sydney. It is significant that the American Revolution came at such a time that Americans could borrow heavily from English political philosophers and the philosophers of the Enlightenment and too early for Americans to be much influenced by Rousseau and the romantic movement.

There were not many men, of course, who studied Greek and Roman philosophers and historians and the works of Milton, Harrington, Locke, and Montesquieu. But a few of them plowed deep, seeking knowledge that would help meet the emergencies and solve the problems of their day. Through the conversations and writings of these few, especially by means of the Virginia Bill of Rights and the Declaration of Independence as well as other public papers, men in general became familiar with such doctrines as the equality of men before the law, the right of each man to life, liberty, and property, and the right of a nation of men to overthrow an oppressive government and establish another in its stead. Out of English history and the contemporary doctrines of the Enlightenment Virginians found help in meeting present problems in their belief that there were natural laws above and independent of man-made law; that natural law was benevolent; that man if not perfectible was at least improvable; and that knowledge and reason were the tools to be used in shaping a better government and society. And their faith in these things was a spur toward realizing a better day.

Above all, it was the Revolution which drove many Americans to deep and sober thought. As events led toward the decision to attempt independence, they thought much about such fundamental problems as the relationship of parts to the whole in political organizations, of the balance of liberty and authority, of the possibility that a severing of the ties with the stabilizing force of British government might entail economic collapse and social disintegration. Walking close along the brink of chaos, thoughtful and responsible men were forced to think seriously about the nature of society and government.

Toward England, the planter-statesmen of Virginia were revolutionists, but toward the forms of government that they had in large measure inherited from England they were conservatives. Possessing an extra measure of power, they showed no disposition to change the arrangements which gave them that power. But some of their non-political privileges they did relinquish. These landholding, slaveholding members of the Established Church planned and in large measure executed a group of reforms that separated church and state, provided a more intelligent and humane criminal code, and moved toward a more equitable distribution of land. And some of them gave serious thought to the abolition of slavery.

Jefferson believed that the Revolution set the stage for this reform movement by compelling men to shift their eyes from private gain to general welfare. Toward the end of the conflict he wrote: "The time for fixing every essential right on a legal basis is while our rulers are honest, and ourselves united. From the conclusion of this war we shall be going down hill. ... [The people] will forget themselves, but in the sole faculty of making money." [5] Long after the event, Jefferson made another observation about the effect of the Revolution on his generation. An enthusiastic young idealist asked him to lead a crusade against slavery and offered to enlist under the banner. Jefferson answered that the cause was good but that he was old and infirm. Leadership belonged to younger men. He added this trenchant remark: "I have outlived the generation with which mutual labors and perils begat mutual confidence and influence." [6]

The Revolution left marks on the spirits and souls of men; and it revealed men to each other. A man's courage or cowardice, his strength and weaknesses, his willingness or unwillingness to sacrifice for the common cause were not easily concealed when men had to take sides and assume unusual responsibilities. Subsequently the men of the Revolution could work together with extraordinary knowledge about the character, attitudes, and capacities of each other. Often they would disagree, but seldom would they misjudge or misunderstand one another.

Good fortune in family environment and traditions, superior educational advantages, familiarity with the energizing political philosophy of the Enlightenment, responsibilities of plantation management, and the thought-provoking experience of living in a revolutionary period were among the circumstances that made Jefferson, Washington, Madison, Mason, and their colleagues into persons who were fit for high political responsibility. But these were not the forces that put these men into office. The characteristics and manners of voters and candidates, the powers of the important offices and governing bodies of Virginia, the written law and the unwritten code of political behavior—these established a discriminating set of processes that sifted through the whole population, discarding most men while selecting for political preferment those few who are now called the great generation of Virginians.

CHAPTER TWO

Tumults and Riots

O N THE twenty-fifth of March, 1756, the customary
procedure of organizing an assembly of the Province
of Virginia was acted out in the Capitol at Williamsburg. In
the elegantly furnished council chamber on the second floor
Governor Robert Dinwiddie sat with the members of his
Council. In the first-floor room of the opposite wing, eighty-
five newly elected burgesses assembled and took their oaths.
This done they received the Governor's command to attend
him in the council chamber. Having climbed the stairs they
stood before him, for there was no room for them to sit, to
hear him utter the single sentence: "Gentlemen of the House
of Burgesses, You must return again to your House, and
immediately proceed to the Choice of a Speaker." [1] The burgesses returned and on nomination by Landon Carter chose
John Robinson. Then they rejoined the Governor and Council
and notified him of their action.

All the while Governor and burgesses were playing their
respective parts in these time-honored ceremonies, they were
eyeing each other with cautious hostility. Four months earlier
the vigorous and able but tactless Dinwiddie had dissolved the
Assembly because of the "troublesome and factious" behavior
of the members. He had hoped, doubtless, that a general election would return a more docile House; but what he saw when

the burgesses and their Speaker crowded before him in the small council chamber was not encouraging. Nearly two thirds of the members and nearly all of the leaders of the former House were back. And the burgesses had reelected their former Speaker by unanimous vote.[2]

As the representative of the Crown and the representatives of the people faced each other, Speaker Robinson petitioned the Governor on behalf of the burgesses "That they might enjoy their ancient Rights and Privileges, such as Freedom of Speech, and Debate, Exemptions from Arrests, and Protections for their Estates." Dinwiddie responded "That he should take Care to defend them in all their just Rights and Privileges."[3] The form of this petition and response had long since been set by tradition, but the tensions of the moment gave to the ancient words a vital and timely meaning.

Fortunately for the Governor, the next step in the customary procedure was his speech to the House. Having the initiative, he could introduce topics for consideration that might draw the attention of the burgesses away from their former quarrel with him. He reminded them in this speech that the French were threatening British power in America and that their Indian allies were endangering the lives of Virginians along the western frontier. He spoke of councils of war and of the need of cooperation with the northern colonies. He recommended "the Arming of the Militia, and to have their Arms of one Bore," because "great Inconveniences may occur by having Guns of Different Bores." Since it was now the end of March and a campaign was being planned for the summer, he urged the House "with all imaginable Dispatch" to make "an immediate effectual Provision of Men and Money for the Expedition against the *French* Encroachments."[4]

Although the House found time to make "Provision against Invasions and Insurrections," and "for the better Protection of the Inhabitants on the Frontiers of this Colony," [5] its immediate response to the urgent pleas of the Governor was a clear notice, given by deed rather than in words, that it would retreat not one whit from the defense of its rights and privileges and that it intended to do little business at this session. It made this plain by appointing none of the customary standing committees except the Committee of Privileges and Elections and by filling this large committee, which was the guardian of the rights and privileges of the House, with some of the ablest and most powerful of the burgesses.

It was well for the House to guard carefully its own rights and privileges, for more was at stake than the vanity of the members and the prestige of the House. The House of Burgesses was the only elected body in colonial Virginia. On the success of the burgesses in their stand against the Governor and on their good management of burgess elections depended the continuance of self-government in Virginia. Supervision over these two important matters was entrusted especially to the Committee of Privileges and Elections.

The Committee was expected to gaze unblinkingly with a cold and suspicious eye on the doings of the Governor and Council at the other end of the Capitol. On occasion the monotony of defensive watchfulness was broken by an aggressive invasion of the Governor's domain. There was a dramatic moment during this session when the House sent its mace-bearer over to the Council, which was then sitting as the General Court of Virginia, and even into the bar of that court, to fetch some of its officials who were members of the House. The outraged Governor publicly expressed his "Resentment at the great Indignity offered the Supream Court of this Colony." [6]

The other and the more time-consuming of the functions of the Committee of Privileges and Elections was to examine the credentials of members of the House, to investigate disputed elections, and to supervise in minute detail the processes by which burgesses were elected. The matters before this Committee must often have seemed petty and wearisome, but if the exercise of these powers had been allowed to slip into the hands of the Governor, there was every likelihood that he would have been able to influence elections so as to build a strong court party in the House. The notable absence of such a party in Virginia on the eve of the American Revolution indicates how carefully the House had guarded and exercised this power.

The ultimate effects of the work of the Committee of Privileges and Elections were more important than the members perhaps realized. But they understood the immediate significance of what they were doing well enough to make them vigilant and active; and the record of their activities affords deep insight into those processes by which men rose to power in colonial Virginia.

The first step in burgess elections was the issuance of a writ from the Governor ordering an election. [7] In general elections, two burgesses were to be chosen from each county and one each from Jamestown, Williamsburg, Norfolk, and the College of William and Mary. Special elections were ordered from time to time to fill a single seat vacated by death, expulsion of a member from the House, or otherwise. The writ was directed to the sheriff, and it was returnable by a date, usually six or eight weeks later, indicated in the document. [8] Upon receiving the writ, the sheriff decided the time for holding the election, which was usually several weeks in the future and on a county-court day. To give public notice of the election, he delivered copies of the writ, with the time and place endorsed thereon, to the parish minister and to the readers of the churches and chapels in the county whose duty it was to publish this information at the close of divine service each Sunday until election day. After the election was held, the sheriff attached to the writ a certificate containing the names of those who had been elected and transmitted these documents to the House.[9]

The Committee of Privileges and Elections examined these papers and reported its findings to the House. Those that were in good order, the House approved. Minor irregularities were amended by the clerk on order of the House. In a few cases the Committee recommended that the sergeant-at-arms take the sheriff into custody and bring him to the House to amend his faulty return or to answer questions concerning the conduct of the election.[10] The investigation of improperly conducted elections and of disputed elections constituted the most critical part of the Committee's work.

Within the first week of this session in 1756 the Committee brought to the attention of the House an Augusta County election that had been conducted improperly. James Lockart, sheriff, returned the election writ with a letter, dated December 17, 1755, explaining that although he had used all the means in his power to hold the election, "the People were so tumultuous and riotous, that I could not finish the Poll; for which Reason no Burgesses could be returned for the said County."[11]

When this matter was reported to the House, the House at once ordered Lockart, who was standing all the while at the door, to be brought by the sergeant-at-arms to the bar "to give an account of the chief Movers in the Tumult and Riot." At the bar, "being examined by the Speaker from the Chair," he declared that "the chief Movers of the said Tumult and Riot" were Richard Woods, David Cloyd, and Joseph Lapsley. The House thereupon resolved that they were "guilty of a Breach of the Privilges of this House," and it ordered them to answer for their offense. Their answer was in the form of a petition asserting their innocence. Woods piously said that "so far from being concerned in, or encouraging the Tumult," he "often applied to the Sheriff, desiring him to command Assistance to suppress the same, and offering his own Assistance therein." [12]

After some investigation, the Committee of Privileges and Elections reported "that there appears to be great Contrariety of Evidence in this Case." Unable to reconstruct a clear account of what had happened, the Committee gave both versions of the story, beginning with that told by Woods, Cloyd, and Lapsley. It was as follows: "on the 17th day of *December*, 1755, the Day appointed for Election of Burgesses for the said County of *Augusta* to serve in this present General Assembly, the Poll was taken till towards the Evening, when the People crowded into the Court-House and pressed upon the Sheriff, who struck several of the Freeholders with his Staff on the Shins, and pushed them with the same in the Breast and other Parts of the Body, and threatened to push it down their Throats if they did not keep back. That he was desired to summon a Guard to keep the Crowd off, and that the Petitioner *Woods* offered to be one of the Guard: That the Sheriff whispered to several Freeholders as they came to vote to know who they were for, and then refused to take their Votes: That he several Times during the Election left the Court-House, which stopped the same while he was out: That after Candles were lighted the Petitioners *Lapsley* and *Cloyd* came to give their Votes, and the Sheriff seized *Lapsley* by the Breast and pushed him backwards on a Bench, upon which *Cloyd*, with some Warmth, said, 'Collar me too Sir;' that *Lapsley* and *Cloyd* then gave in their Votes, and the Poll was continued some Time afterwards."

The sheriff's story, as might be expected, was somewhat different. He declared: "That while the Poll was taking the Petitioner *Lapsley* pulled out his Purse in the Court-Yard and offered to wager that Mr. *Preston* and Mr. *Alexander*, two of the Candidates, would go Burgesses, and that he and his Party would carry the Day; and that the Petitioner *Woods* was noisy and loud in the Interest of Mr. *Alexander* and offered to wager as *Lapsley* did: That when the crowd pressed on the Sheriff he endeavoured to keep them back in a civil Manner, by putting his Stick a-cross their Breasts, and summoned a Guard to assist him, which was broke thro': That a Person came out of the Court-House and said to *Cloyd*, 'The Election is going against us,' who answered, 'It should not, if we cannot carry it one Way we will have it another: I will put a Stop to the Election;' and immediately the Crowd encreased: That when *Lapsley* pressed thro' the Crowd to give his Vote the Sheriff desired him to keep back, but he pushed on and seized the Sheriff and pushed him against the Table: That after *Lapsley* and *Cloyd* had voted, the Sheriff desired them to withdraw, which they did not do, and in a short Time afterwards the Candles were struck out by the Petitioner *Woods*, and the Riot began which put an End to the Election, the Sheriff being thrown on the Table, which broke under him, and the Clerks fled to the Bench; and during the Tumult

Lapsley called out, 'Lads, Stand by me. I'll pay the Fine, cost what it will: You know I am able.' " [13]

On the Committee's recommendation, the House ordered Woods, Cloyd, and Lapsley to pay the charges and expenses to which the sheriff had been put, and it requested the Governor to issue a new writ for electing burgesses for the County of Augusta.[14]

Though eighteenth-century elections were seldom so turbulent as this election in the frontier village of Augusta Court House, they were usually lively and exciting. The voters came by horseback and wagon from all over the county, many of them having left home that morning though a few spent the night with friends or with one of the candidates who lived along the road. In the larger counties some of the voters had to ride twenty-five miles or more to an election.[15]

The election was held at a single place in each county, and the law required that it be held at the courthouse, though unusual circumstances, such as the outbreak of smallpox at Fredericksburg, the county seat of Spotsylvania, might cause the sheriff to choose another place.[16] Many of the voters would have been at the courthouse on the appointed day had there been no election, for elections were generally set on county-court days when men assembled to transact business connected with the court, to buy and sell land, slaves, and other commodities, to catch up on the news, and to enjoy the excitement and activity of court day. In eighteenth-century Virginia elections, the plentiful supplies of liquor, occasional fights, and "drunken loungers at and about the Courthouses" marred the assemblages of "the good people and the industrious." [17] A traveler through Virginia in 1778 wrote this amusing description of his experiences at Hanover Court House on election day: "The moment I alighted [from the stage], a wretched pug-nosed fellow assailed me, to swap watches. I had hardly shaken him off, when I was attacked by a wild Irishman, who insisted on my 'swapping horses' with him; and, in a twinkling ran up the pedigree of his horse to the grand-dam. Treating his importunity with little respect, I was near being involved in a boxing-match, the Irishman swearing that I did not 'trate him like a jintleman.' I had hardly escaped this dilemma, when my attention was attracted to a fight between two very unwieldy, fat men, foaming and puffing like two furies, until one succeeded in twisting his forefinger in a side-lock of the other's hair, and was in the act of thrusting, by this purchase, his thumb into his adversary's eye, when he bawled out 'King's cruse,' equivalent, in technical language, to 'enough.' " [18]

The election was usually held in the courtroom, though sometimes in good weather it was moved out to the courthouse green. Activity centered about a long table. Behind it sat the sheriff, or in his rare absence an under-sheriff. He was usually flanked by several of the ranking justices of the county, and at the extreme ends sat the candidates. Near at hand were the clerks or "writers" of the candidates, who sometimes reimbursed their clerical assistants handsomely. George Washington's expenses in an election to the House of Burgesses on December 1, 1768, included an item of £1 to "John Orr [for] keeping my Poll at the Election." [19] Before the voting began, each clerk wrote at the top of a sheet of paper the name of his candidate. The poll sheets used in an election in Northumberland County on July 19, 1758, bore the following headings: "A Poll Taken by Col. Presly Thornton," "A Poll Taken for Col. Spencer Ball," and "A Poll Taken for Mr. Robert Clarke." The paper was ruled and the lines numbered so that one could tell at a glance at any moment in the election "exactly how many votes each candidate had.[20] A less common system of recording votes was to write the names of the voters on the left side of the sheet and to indicate their preferences by check marks or otherwise in columns prepared on the right side of the sheet, each column being headed by the name of one of the candidates.[21] When the sheriff thought that all was in readiness, which was likely to be mid-morning after most of the voters had had time to assemble,[22] he opened the election by reading the writ which ordered it. In case there were no more candidates than there were places to be filled or in case sentiment was very one-sided, the law allowed the election to be determined "by view." Whether the decision was reached in such a case by a show of hands or by some other method is not revealed in the records. George Washington was elected burgess without a poll on September 14, 1769.[23] Delegates of Orange County to the state legislature were chosen by view on April 24, 1799.[24]

When a poll was taken—and election by poll seems to have been more frequent than by view—the voters presented themselves one by one before the table where the election officials sat. Voters were not registered before elections, and there were no officials to turn back nonqualified men before they reached the polling place. However, the sheriff could refuse to take the vote of a man whom he knew to be disqualified, and each candidate had the right to challenge any voter and to require that he swear that he met the legal requirements. Objections could be entered by the names of doubtful voters to serve as a beginning point for a House of Burgesses investigation in case the election was contested. The most common objection was "no freehold." Others were "under 21 years old," "not a citizen of ... Virginia or of the United States," and "Joseph Carter, Jr., Sheriff of Lancaster, not a right to vote as he did."

During an election in Westmoreland County on May 24, 1748, Captain Robert Quarles objected to a good many men who voted for John Bushrod and George Lee. On second thought Quarles, who trailed his nearest competitor by 44 votes, seems to have decided that it was useless to take his case to the House. It is unlikely that he could have proved that more than 44 voters had no right to vote.[25]

The candidates were not disposed to challenge doubtful voters unless much was at stake, for insistence on a rigid enforcement of the law might turn public opinion against them. In Lunenburg County some forty men who could not qualify were allowed to vote in an election held in 1771. By common consent and contrary to the law, a local movement toward universal manhood suffrage was on foot.[26]

As each freeholder came before the sheriff, his name was called out in a loud voice, and the sheriff inquired how he would vote. The freeholder replied by giving the name of his preference. The appropriate clerk then wrote down the voter's name, the sheriff announced it as enrolled, and often the candidate for whom he had voted arose, bowed, and publicly thanked him.[27] When a voter came before the table in the contest for a seat in Congress between John Marshall and John Clopton in 1799, the sheriff asked: "Mr. Blair, who do you vote for?" "John Marshall," said he; and thereupon the future Chief Justice of the United States replied: "Your vote is appreciated, Mr. Blair." As the next voter approached, the sheriff inquired: "Who do you vote for, Mr. Buchanan?" "For John Clopton," he answered; and Clopton, at the other end of the table, responded: "Mr. Buchanan, I shall treasure that vote in my memory. It will be regarded as a feather in my cap for ever." [28]

When the going was close, as it was in this election, there were feverish efforts to bring in a few more voters who would poll on the "right" side. Marshall's Federalist supporters with great effort persuaded the Episcopal clergyman and his good friend the Presbyterian minister to come to the election in the closing moments; but those two worthies maintained the political neutrality of the cloth by voting, one for Marshall and the other for Clopton.

A notably close election occurred in Elizabeth City County in 1762, with both sides doing their best to round up every possible voter. James Wallace, who was defeated by the narrow margin of two votes, charged that William Wager, his successful opponent, had brought men to the polls who had no right to vote; and he therefore challenged Wager's right to a seat in the House of Burgesses. The Committee of Privileges and Elections made a thorough investigation of the property-holdings of some of the voters and ordered several names struck from the poll sheets. The Committee also investigated the sanity of old Mr. William Tucker. His vote was challenged because for "7 or 8 Years past" he had "been generally reputed not to have been in his proper Senses." Evidence of his dotage, among other things, was the fact that he had "sometimes met with his old Acquaintances, whom he hath not known, and particularly met with one *William Face* in the Street, invited him home with him, and when he was there asked him who he was." Nevertheless, his mind seems to have been clear on election day, "which is plain from his inquiring of the Person that was sent for him to attend the Election who was ahead, and being answered that the sitting Member was behind, he immediately called for his Stick, and on his Way to the Court House, having dropped one of his Shoes, he desired to be set down in the Chair in which he was carried to have it put on again, and that when at the Court House he gave his Vote distinctly for the sitting Member and one *John Jones,* and repeated it, though in a low Voice." After hearing all the evidence, the House decided that Tucker had a "good Right" to vote.

In this case the House was also asked to review the manner in which the sheriff had conducted the election, and especially his decision as to closing it. According to law, he was to conclude the election whenever all the voters present had exercised their right of suffrage. In this election, so it was alleged, a proposal was made to the sheriff "with the Approbation and Consent of all the Candidates ... to postpone closing the Poll until Sunsetting." The sheriff agreed, and thereupon Dr. John Brodie, "with some other Freeholders, went out of Town, in Order to bring in 2 other Freeholders ... to give their Votes at the said Election." But the sheriff, "soon after the said Agreement among the Candidates and himself, received and polled two Voters for the sitting Member, and 1 for the Petitioner, closed the Poll, which was about an Hour and a Half before Sunset, notwithstanding the earnest Intreaties of the Petitioner and some of his Friends, ... to whom the Sheriff made Answer, 'that he knew his Duty, and should not be directed by him, and that he should close the Poll when he thought proper.'" One of the two freeholders who were on their way to vote was near enough "to be able to distinguish the sitting Member carried off through the Streets by the Populace." [29]

The excitement and tension of close elections was enhanced

by oral voting. Simply by listening, one could tell fairly well how things were going. By looking over the shoulders of the clerks, an exact check on the standing of the candidates could be made at any moment. As first one and then another forged ahead, each voter was heard with breathless interest. When he had spoken, there were huzzas and shouts of approval from one side answered by scowls and sharp retorts from the disappointed. Wagers were offered and accepted, and fights sometimes broke out.[30] In the heat of a Lunenburg County election a man by the name of John Hobson resorted to behavior "which was very illegal and tumuluous, in offering to lay Wagers the Poll was closed when it was not; in proclaiming at the Court-house Door the Poll was going to be closed, and desiring Freeholders to come in and vote, and then violently, by striking and kicking of them, preventing them from so doing, by which Means many Freeholders did not vote at the said Election." For this "Breach of the Privileges and Freedom of Elections, and also the Privileges" of the House of Burgesses, Hobson was brought to the bar to state "that if his Zeal to serve his friends on that Occasion led him into any indiscreet Actions, he is heartily sorry for the same, and humbly begs Pardon of this House for his Offence."[31]

George Washington was at the center of an angry scene during an election in Fairfax County on December 11, 1755. So close was this contest that the leading candidate had only 12 votes more than the lowest, the final vote standing John West 232, George William Fairfax 222, and William Ellzey 220. Washington, already a colonel though only twenty-three years old, was for Fairfax, to whom he was bound by ties of friendship as well as by calculations of political advantage. At some time during the day he came face to face with William

Payne, who was working against Fairfax. Strong words must have been spoken by Washington, for Payne, a smaller man, knocked him down with his stick. There was talk of a duel, but next day Washington apologized for what he had said and friendly relations were resumed.[32] Although fights and riots sometimes occurred, many elections were conducted with dignity and decorum. It was remarked of an election at Alexandria on July 14, 1774, when Washington was a candidate, that "the Poll was over in about two hours and conducted with great order and regularity." [33]

When the sheriff decided that all of the freeholders present had voted in an election, he went to the door of the courthouse and called out three times: "Gentlemen freeholders, come into court, and give your votes, or the poll will be closed." [34] The decision to close the polls was solely the sheriff's with no appeal except to the House of Burgesses. The election might be ended as early as two o'clock in the afternoon, it might continue until after candles were lit, or it might last for more than one day in case the electors were too numerous to be polled in a day or if many of them had been kept away "by rain or rise of watercourses." A snow storm in the spring of 1821 kept many voters from the polls in one of the Virginia counties. At the next legislature a bill was introduced, but it did not pass, to add snow storms to the list of occurrences that would justify an extension of the election period.[35] Because of bad weather an Orange County election begun on April 27, 1795, was not concluded until the next day; [36] but it was rare for elections to last more than one day, and voters usually knew the outcome before starting back to their farms and plantations.

The polling being over, each clerk signed his record of the voting under oath that it had been correctly made, the sheriff announced the results, and if feeling was high the winning candidates were carried off on the shoulders of their friends or in "chairs, raised aloft by the free-holders." [37] Sometimes the day ended with a ball or supper or other celebration. [38] The poll sheets were filed with the county clerk to be examined by anyone who cared to do so, and the sheriff made the returns to the House of Burgesses.

Washington, Jefferson, Madison, Henry, Marshall, Mason, Monroe, and nearly every other Virginian of political importance in the eighteenth and early nineteenth centuries participated time and again as voter and as candidate in this kind of election, which changed little so long as any of them lived. They did not necessarily approve of every feature of this way of choosing representatives, but when they thought or spoke of popular elections their minds must have turned to the county courts on election days. To understand their handiwork in establishing American representative government and their thoughts about the philosophy and ideals of democracy one must remember that behind their thoughts and deeds lay their own experiences in Virginia politics as well as their reading from such authors as Harrington, Locke, and Montesquieu.

In addition to teaching these men something about politics, burgess elections played a part in giving them the power to put their ideas into effect. At this time politics was so constructed that scarcely any Virginian reached a high political position in state or nation without first serving in the Assembly. Burgess elections were thus a part of the selective process that vested these men with the power to make effective whatever convictions they had about government.

CHAPTER THREE

The Vulgar Herd

AS EACH VOTER came before the sheriff to proclaim his preference among the candidates, he held for one brief moment the center of the political stage. Then at least he felt that he counted for something in government. Those who watched the procession of voters—plain farmers and periwigged gentlemen, the young man voting for the first time and the old man hobbling up with his cane, the blusterer who spoke loudly and the timid man who would have preferred a secret ballot—had a passing show of the variety of personalities at the core of Virginia politics.

Each candidate must have watched the scene and heard the words of the voters with intense interest. His political fate was being settled, and his campaign methods were being subjected to the acid test. He must often have wished that he had conducted himself differently during the days before the election or that he had said more or different words to individual voters. If he stood for office again, he probably modified his tactics according to what he had learned in his earlier effort to win support.

The habits, manners, and attitudes of these men who came to the polls played a part in determining the nature of political leadership in eighteenth-century Virginia. The successful candidate was a man who understood the voters and who was willing and able to practice the arts by which their approval could be won. He was not necessarily like the men who elected him, but he had to possess qualities that they approved.

There was little change through the eighteenth and the early part of the nineteenth centuries in the legal description of the Virginia voter. Indians and Negroes, whether free or slave, were disfranchised.[1] Nor could women vote. Suffrage was granted only to white males, twenty-one years old and over, who could meet a landholding qualification and, through the colonial period, a religious qualification.

Under the colonial laws, no recusant was supposed to vote or hold office. A strict interpretation of this rule would have excluded from the polls and from office all who did not adhere to the Established Church; but, as a matter of fact, dissenters seem to have voted freely in the late-colonial period. The law itself recognized Quakers as voters, for it allowed them to meet one of the requirements by making affirmation instead of by oath.[2] The candidates cultivated the good will of dissenters with great zeal. A candidate for burgess in Hanover County decided at a critical stage of his campaign that the church for him to attend was "the lower Meeting House of the Dissenters."[3] In Albemarle, a dozen Presbyterians rode to the home of a neighbor to persuade him to become a candidate.[4] Many Scotch-Irish and German names on the poll lists of Frederick County suggest that a large number of dissenters were voting in that county. It is certain that such well-known nonconformists as the Reverend John Hoge, a Presbyterian,[5] and the Reverend John Alderson, a Baptist, voted in 1758.[6]

The weight of election statistics supports the belief that dissenters voted freely. If Jefferson were anywhere near correct in his estimate that "two-thirds of the people had become dissenters at the commencement of the present revolution," [7] and if the dissenters had been disfranchised, there obviously would have been a great upsurge in the number of votes after religious restrictions were abolished in 1785. Instead, the records of a considerable number of county elections show that the average number of votes was not much affected, and was certainly not increased, by the passage of this law.[8]

The landholding requirement, which changed but little in a hundred years, was a much more important restriction on voting. After 1736 a man could vote if for a year before the election he had owned 25 acres "with a house and plantation" upon it or 100 acres of unoccupied land, or if he had owned a house and lot in one of the towns. In the year 1785 the minimum of unsettled land was reduced from 100 acres to 50 acres; [9] but, instead of helping the poor farmer, who ordinarily qualified with the small tract on which he lived, this change probably did more to make it easier for the wealthy planter to qualify in several counties. In some instances residents of towns could vote without owning property; and, in general, townsmen met with more generous suffrage provisions than did countrymen.[10] With less than 12,000 white persons living in the nine Virginia towns in 1790 this was, however, an insignificant matter.[11]

When Jefferson was a young man, most of the Virginia voters qualified by owning the 25 or more acres of land on which they lived. In 1785 the minimum size of the dwelling which the voter had to have on his 25 acres or his town lot was for the first time clearly prescribed. A definite rule was needed, for colonial Virginians sometimes tried to qualify with strange habitations. David Curle, who owned 86 acres in Elizabeth City County, voted in an election in 1756 because there was a house "25 Feet by 15" on his land. But the house was "much out of Repair, most Part of the Weather-Boards being off and Part of the Shingles, and the Sills rotten." It was uninhabitable, and no one had lived in it for several years.[12]

Six years later Thomas Payne of the same county voted in an election on the strength of a dubious title to a remarkable house. On the Saturday before the election he had purchased "for the Value of 10 s. a small House, about 4 and Half Feet Pitch, 4 or 5 Feet long, and 2 or 2 and a Half Feet wide, floored or laid with Plank in the midst of its Height, to put Milkpans, or other Things, on; and . . . he had the same removed in a Cart, with one Horse, with the Assistance of 7 or 8 Men, and placed on his said Lot, on Purpose (as he acknowledged) to qualify him to vote at that Election." After the election was over, the woman from whom he had purchased this little structure, "being in Doubt whether she should get her Money of him for the said House, had the same removed home again." [13] The House of Burgesses decided that neither Curle nor Payne was qualified to vote, and it ordered their names struck from the poll sheets. In the same year that Payne's case was decided, the burgesses passed an act making twelve feet square the minimum size for an occupied house, whether on farm or town lot, to qualify the owner to vote. But this act of 1762 was not confirmed in England and did not become law until 1785.[14]

Since land was relatively cheap and the house on it needed to be nothing more than a one-room log cabin, a man did not have to be rich or even well-to-do to qualify as a voter. The valuation for tax purposes of most twenty-five-acre holdings in the 1780's was between five and fifteen pounds.[15] Whether the house was occupied by the owner or a tenant, the vote belonged to the owner. Unless the tenant owned land in his own name he had no legal right to vote, and there is very little evidence that landless tenants voted in the last half of the eighteenth century.[16]

Such were the rules that determined who could vote. There is no way of knowing exactly how many qualified under these rules, how many white males of voting age there were in Virginia, or how many of the qualified voters actually went to the polls; but an attempt must be made, difficult as it is, to reach approximate answers to these questions.

The total number of Virginians in the year 1790 was 747,610, of whom 442,117 were white. The number of white males was 227,071. The Federal census of 1790, from which these figures were taken, does not show how many of these were of voting age, but they probably numbered between 90,000 and 100,000.[17] Many of these were kept from voting by the propertyholding requirement. Jefferson estimated that more than half of the "free and adult male citizens" were thus disqualified.[18] Governor Robert Dinwiddie and St. George Tucker, in contrast, thought that a majority of the white men of Virginia could vote,[19] and there were other and widely varying opinions.[20]

Statistics support Jefferson rather than Tucker and Dinwiddie. There were, of course, no official registration lists, but because the right to vote depended on owning a minimum amount of taxable real estate, the land-tax lists should contain the names of all who were entitled to vote. These lists were often used by the Committee of Privileges and Elections of the House of Burgesses when investigating disputed elections.

Seven counties—Albemarle, Buckingham, Culpeper, Essex, Orange, Princess Anne, and Stafford—have been chosen for a sample count of the number of landowners. They were selected because for them, and only for them, were records found of the number of men who voted in one or more elections in the 1780's. In these counties there were 4,298 landowners in the late 1780's, not counting orphans, women, or estates. Only 56 of this number, less than 1.5 per cent, owned fewer than 25 acres. There were not many more on the lists who owned between 25 and 50 acres.[21] Evidently, the amount of property required for voting was small enough to enfranchise nearly all white male landowners; the law did not keep great numbers of small, independent farmers from voting.

If the ratio of qualified voters to total white males was the same in all Virginia as it was in these seven counties, 41,942 was the maximum vote that might have been given in the state in the year 1790.[22] Of course this number is much too exact, and it is certainly too large; for some of the 25-acre holdings must have lacked houses, and some men owned land in two or more counties. However, it is probably safe to say that between 35,000 and 40,000 men—between a third and a half of the adult white male population—were qualified to vote at this time. The available evidence indicates that almost half of the qualified voters came to the polls and voted. In thirteen elections held in the seven sample counties between the years 1786 and 1789, about 48.1 per cent of the qualified voters actually voted.

By law all freeholders were required to vote in elections. He who failed to vote in the county where he lived and owned property was subject to a penalty which was set in the year 1662 at 200 pounds of tobacco to be collected with costs by any informant.[23] After 1785 the delinquent voter was supposed to forfeit an amount equal to one-fourth of his levies and taxes for the year. The presiding magistrate of each county was required to charge the grand jury to present all qualified voters who had failed to participate in the previous election. To aid in discovering these persons, the law provided that the jury be given a list of the freeholders and a copy of the poll.

The new law seems to have been no better enforced than the old one. When the grand jury of Amherst County presented more than 75 men "for not Attending and Voting, at the Election of Delegates," the county court dismissed the case.[24] When the Mecklenburg court imposed fines upon 510 freeholders in 1793, the freeholders made an appeal to the governor in which they explained that some of them had not received notice of the election and that most of them were farmers and planters who "could not attend the election without manifest injury to their crops." They declared that the law had hitherto been unenforced in Mecklenburg County, and that "the Grand Juries of no adjacent County have enforced the law."[25] The voters continued to consult personal convenience, the weather, and the distance to the polls in deciding whether to attend elections after 1785 just as they had done in the last decade of the colonial period when some of the freeholders of Hanover County declared that "it was too cold Weather to go so long a Way (it being above 25 Miles) to the election."[26]

There is every reason to accept St. George Tucker's generalization that "Except on some great occasion where a contest may happen, between influential persons, the whole body of freeholders in a county, rarely, perhaps, never, attend."[27] How else could one explain the fact that whereas 400 men voted in Essex County in 1788 for representatives to the legislature, only 19 voted four years later in a presidential election, and 393 voted the following year for a congressman? [28]

The laws also allowed some men to vote in more than one constituency. The president and professors of the College of William and Mary not only voted for burgesses to represent James City County but also elected one burgess to represent the College; [29] and, if they owned a house and lot in the town of Williamsburg, they could vote for a representative of the city as well. Without changing his residence George Wythe successively represented all three of these constituencies between 1754 and 1768: the City of Williamsburg, the College of William and Mary, and Elizabeth City County. But the door through which the largest number of men came to the polls in the same election a second, third, or fourth time was the provision, which remained in force until 1851, that a man could vote in every county in which he owned enough land to qualify. Naturally, he had to overcome the physical handicap of distance and slow transportation, but in the colonial period he did not have to do all of his voting within a single day. Election day varied from county to county, and occasionally a county election lasted more than one day. Even after election days were made uniform over the state in the early national period, it was still possible for a man of determination and physical stamina to reach two or more of the county seats in a single day. There is a tradition that in the late antebellum period a Virginian prided himself on voting in four counties, a feat which he accomplished by arranging relays of horses at county seats. [30]

The exact number of men who could vote in two or more

constituencies can not be known, but they were certainly numerous enough to be a significant force in politics. At a poll taken in Essex County in 1824, eight of the 131 votes were cast by non-residents.[31] In Fauquier County, where 399 votes were given in an election in the year 1769, some 70 non-residents were qualified to vote, though for one reason or another many of them took no part in this election.[32] It is reasonable to suppose that non-resident voting was heavier in close, critical elections, and that this multiplication of political power was enjoyed by rich men rather than by poor.

What manner of men were the disfranchised? A few were overseers, but all overseers were not without land of their own. Others were tenants, more numerous, perhaps, in the Northern Neck than elsewhere,[33] and farm managers or laborers who owned no land. Examples of such persons, men who were old enough to vote but who could not because they were landless, were recorded as a result of a law of 1784 which imposed a tax upon all white males above the age of 21.[34] For instance, Eliza Bradley, of Charles City County, who owned 300 acres, paid the tax for James Hamblet, who had no land and who probably cultivated or managed the cultivation of her land. Similarly, John Colgin with 596 acres paid the tax for Philip Bullivant, and William Clark with 219 acres paid the tax for Joseph Hilliard.[35] In addition to these disfranchised men of the soil, there must have been artisans, craftsmen, professional men, and merchants and their employees who were landless; and doubtless there were unfortunate men as well as shiftless men who never secured enough land to vote.

A large number of the disfranchised white men were adult sons of landowners. If a father could spare the land and saw any good reason for enfranchising his son, he could, of course, deed him enough land to make him a voter and therefore qualify him to hold office.[36] But most fathers, so it seems, were not disposed to divide their land with their grown sons, and often the family holding was too small to be made into two farms. The tax lists are full of cases like that of William Kent, Jr., who could not vote though his father owned 85 acres in Northumberland County, or like William Edwards, Jr., and James Bullivant, Jr., of Charles City County, who were landless though their fathers owned 50 acres and 219 acres respectively.[37] These and other landless young men could expect some day to qualify as voters by inheritance if they did not first secure land by purchase or marriage dowry. Because of the numerous instances of this kind it follows that estimates of the per cent of adult white men who were disfranchised at any one time present the facts in an unfavorable light. It must be remembered that a good number of the white males who could not vote at the age of twenty-one could vote by the time they were thirty or forty years old.

Landholding was a requirement for voting, but this requirement was only a symbol and formal statement of something more fundamental. What the early Virginians were trying to do was to give the vote to those men, and only those men, who gave, as they expressed it in their first state constitution, "sufficient evidence of permanent common interest with, and attachment to, the community." [38] This goal was not perfectly accomplished by restricting the suffrage to landowners, but it did not miss it far in that day when the great majority of Virginians were farmers and planters. Most men of other occupations—physicians, clergymen, lawyers, teachers, blacksmiths, carpenters, millers, merchants, and storekeepers—lived by payments from the planters and farmers. Their stake in the predominantly agricultural society was indirect but real, and all except the poorest of them could acquire enough land to qualify as voters.

The requirement that a voter must own land was not intended to set off the farmers against the rest of society, nor was its purpose to vest political power in the rich to the exclusion of the poor. The voters, for the most part, were neither great planters nor very poor men. About a fourth of them owned less than 100 acres, a half owned between 100 and 300 acres, and a fourth owned more than 300 acres. Less than one in twenty was master of more than 1000 acres.[39] Probably as many as a third owned no slaves, and there were many others who owned no more than one family of Negroes.[40]

Perhaps the best definition of the Virginia voter in the late colonial and early national periods would omit all details of age, of land ownership, and of other matters and would concentrate on the fact that he was the head of a family.[41] The very poor and some others were excluded, but most of the farmers, small as well as great, were enfranchised. Because farmers lived on their own land, they enjoyed a large measure of independence. The Virginia farmers, even those whose acres were few, could afford to speak their mind on election day with less risk of economic retaliation than could their descendants in the complex and interrelated society and economy of the twentieth century. As heads of families, it was their business to manage their farms or plantations, to care for and support their dependents, black as well as white, and to represent their families in business dealings with the world about them. Such were the persons to whom the vote was given; and when they voted they spoke for their families in much the same way that they acted for their families in selling tobacco, buying supplies, or arranging for the education of their children.

By twentieth-century standards, eighteenth-century Virginia fell far short of perfect democracy. But its imperfections, such as the exclusion of propertyless men from the polls and the requirement that voting be oral, were common elsewhere in that day. Virginia was ahead of Massachusetts and most other parts of America in the late colonial period in percentage of white inhabitants voting in elections.[42] And Virginia was ahead of Americans in many later periods of history in that nearly half of those who were qualified to vote actually participated in elections, and this despite the handicap of having to ride many miles over poor roads to the single polling place in the county.

CHAPTER FOUR

Swilling the Planters with Bumbo

IT WOULD BE pleasant to think that voters were good and wise in the bright, beginning days of the American nation; that in Jefferson's Arcadia, to use a popular euphemism, the sturdy, incorruptible freeholders assembled when occasion demanded and, with an eye only to the public good and their own safety, chose the best and ablest of their number to represent them in the Assembly. It is true that the voters of early Virginia chose their representatives and that often they chose remarkably well; but it is an error to think that the voters were the only positive active force at work in elections. For good or ill, the candidates and their friends also played an important part by using many forms of persuasion and pressure upon the voters.

A play called *The Candidates; or, the Humours of a Virginia Election*, written about 1770 by Colonel Robert Munford of Mecklenburg County, Virginia, provides valuable insight into the part played by candidates in the elections of eighteenth-century Virginia.[1] In this play one of the former delegates to the Assembly, Worthy by name, has decided not to stand for reelection. The other, Wou'dbe, offers himself once more "to the humours of a fickle croud," though with reluctance, asking himself: "Must I again resign my reason, and be nought but what each voter pleases? Must I cajole, fawn, and wheedle, for a place that brings so little profit?" [2] The second candidate, Sir John Toddy, "an honest blockhead," with no ability except in consuming liquor and no political strength except his readiness to drink with the poor man as freely as with the rich, looks for support among the plain people who like him because he "wont turn his back upon a poor man, but will take a chearful cup with one as well as another." [3] Scorned by the leading men of the county, the other two candidates, Smallhopes and Strutabout, a vain, showy fellow, are adept in the low arts of winning the support of ignorant men.

Each of these candidates had some influence, following, or support which, in the language of that day, was known as his interest. It was common practice at this time for two candidates to join interests, as the phrase went, in hopes that each could get the support of the friends of the other. When Sir John suggests to Wou'dbe a joining of interests by asking him "to speak a good word for me among the people," Wou'dbe refuses and tells him plainly "I'll speak a good word to you, and advise you to decline" to run. [4] Because Wou'dbe could not, from principle, join interests with any one of the three other candidates, he loses votes by affronting first one and then another of them. Just in the nick of time, Wou'dbe's colleague Worthy descends from the upper reaches of respectability and greatness to save Wou'dbe from defeat and political virtue from ruin. With stilted phrase Worthy denounces "the scoundrels who opposed us last election" and directs Wou'dbe to "speak this to the people, and let them know I intend to stand a poll." [5] The good men of the county rally to the side

of righteousness; Sir John (between alcoholic hiccoughs) an-
nounces "I'm not so fitten" as "Mr. Worthy and Mr.
Wou'dbe"; Strutabout and Smallhopes, looking as doleful
as thieves upon the gallows, are ignominiously defeated; and
Worthy and Wou'dbe are triumphantly reelected.

Among the more important of the unwritten rules of
eighteenth-century Virginia politics, a rule which the candidates and their advisers often mentioned was the necessity
for candidates to be present at elections. Judge Joseph Jones,
out of his ripe experience, wrote in 1785 to his young nephew
James Monroe, "respecting your offering your service for the
County the coming year,...it would be indispensably necessary you should be in the County before the election and
attend it when made." [6] In 1758 several of Washington's
friends wrote him to "come down" from Fort Cumberland,
where he was on duty with his troops, "and show your face"
in Frederick County where he was a candidate for burgess.
One of his supporters warned him that "you being elected
absolutely depends on your presence." Thanks to the hard
work of his friends and the patriotic circumstances of his
absence, Washington was elected; but it is evident that the
absence of a candidate from the county before and during
the taking of the poll was regarded as a distinct handicap. [7]

Fifty years later Henry St. George Tucker, who planned
to stand for election at Winchester, was delayed by bad
weather and other circumstances at Staunton. He wrote to his
father: "I shall not be able to reach Winchester time enough
for the election and I presume I shall be withdrawn in consequence of what I have written to my friends in Winchester." [8] But by hard driving he made it, arriving "a few
moments before the polls were opened"; and he was elected. [9]

As late as 1815 Tucker continued to place himself personally before the people while the voting was in process. Even though he was "still very weak" from illness, he played his part in an election of that year while the enormous number of 737 votes was polled until, as he wrote his father, "fatigue well nigh overcame me." [10]

A sharp distinction must be made between election-day and pre-election behavior of the candidate toward the voter. The code of the times required that in the days before the election the candidate maintain a dignified aloofness from the voters; however, this rule was broken perhaps as often as it was observed. The tipsy Sir John Toddy, in *The Candidates*, assisted by his henchman Guzzle, tries unabashedly to work himself into the good graces of three freeholders named Prize, Twist, and Stern. As they and their wives are sitting on a rail fence, with other freeholders standing about, Sir John comes up to a group. At his shoulder stands Guzzle to whisper the names of the prospective voters to him.

Sir John. Gentlemen and ladies, your servant, hah! my old friend Prize, how goes it? how does your wife and children do?

Sarah. At your service, sir. (*making a low courtsey.*)

Prize. How the devil come he to know me so well, and never spoke to me before in his life? (*aside.*)

Guzzle. (*whispering to Sir John*) Dick Stern.

Sir John. Hah! Mr. Stern, I'm proud to see you; I hope your family are well; how many children? does the good woman keep to the old stroke?

Catharine. Yes, an't please your honour, I hope my lady's well, with your honour.

Sir John. At your service, madam.

Guzzle. (*whispering* [to] *Sir John*) Roger Twist.

Sir John. Hah! Mr. Roger Twist! your servant, sir. I hope your wife and children are well.

Twist. There's my wife. I have no children, at your service.[11]

James Littlepage, a candidate for burgess in Hanover County in 1763, practiced nearly every art known to his generation for getting his candidacy before the people and winning their support. The gathering of worshippers at church services afforded him an opportunity to meet people; but unfortunately, he could not be at two churches at the same time. Deciding that it was more important to go to a dissenting congregation, he prepared the way by letters to two freeholders in which he announced that he would "be at your Church To-morrow Se'nnight," and asked their support, setting forth the platform on which he was campaigning and circulating the false rumor that his opponent had "declined serving this County."

To take care of matters at the other church which he was unable to attend personally, he sent a letter to three freeholders for them to read and pass about among those in attendance. As one of those who saw the letter recalled its substance, Littlepage wrote that he "was that Day gone to the lower Meeting House of the Dissenters, to know their Sentiments whether they would submit to the damned Tobacco Law, and desired to know whether they also would submit to it; that if they would send him Burgess he would be hanged, or burnt (or Words to that Effect) if he did not get that Part of it, directing a Review of Tobacco, repealed, as being an Infringement on the Liberty of the Subjects, the Inspectors being so intimidated by it that they refused the greater Part of their Tobacco; and that he would endeavor to have the Inspectors chosen by the People."

To meet the voters who could not be found in assemblies, Littlepage went on a house-to-house canvass. After discussing his chances in one part of the county with his friend John Boswell, and being assured that "he might have a good Chance, if he would go up amongst them," Littlepage "accordingly went up, and the said *Boswell* rode about with him among the People." He was the soul of hospitality, inviting those who lived at some distance from the courthouse to spend the night with him on their way to the poll. Littlepage was elected.[12]

James Madison in his old age recalled that when he entered politics it was "the usage for the candidates to recommend themselves to the voters ... by personal solicitation."[13] Madison thoroughly disliked this practice. Shortly before the election of representatives to the first Congress of the United States he wrote from Philadelphia to George Washington: "I am pressed much in several quarters to try the effect of presence on the district into which I fall, for electing a Representative; and am apprehensive that an omission of that expedient, may eventually expose me to blame. At the same time I have an extreme distaste to steps having an electioneering appearance, altho' they should lead to an appointment in which I am disposed to serve the public; and am very dubious moreover whether any step which might seem to denote a solicitude on my part would not be as likely to operate against as in favor of my pretensions." [14]

Colonel Landon Carter, writing in 1776, said that he had

once been "turned out of the H. of B." because "I did not familiarize myself among the People," whereas he well remembered his "son's going amongst them and carrying his Election." The contrasting experiences of father and son suggest that going among the people was important to get a man elected. However, the son, Robert Wormeley Carter, lost his seat in an election in Richmond County in 1776 even though, according to his father, he had "kissed the——of the people, and very seriously accommodated himself to others." With mounting anger the Colonel wrote: "I do suppose such a Circumstance cannot be parallelled, but it is the nature of Popularity. She, I long discovered to be an adultress of the first order." [15] The son was likewise displeased with the decision of the voters, but he naturally thought that his campaign methods were above reproach. He wrote in his diary "as for myself I never ask'd but one man to vote for me since the last Election; by which means I polled but 45. votes an honorable number." [16]

Father and son were miles apart in describing what the son had done; but they were in complete agreement as to what he ought to have done. Both thought that candidates should not solicit votes, and there were other men who thought exactly as they did. Henry St. George Tucker wrote to his father before an election to be held on April 6, 1807, "Please to take notice also, that I am no *electionerer*." "I have studiously avoided anything like canvassing.... My opponents are sufficiently active I learn." Of his victory he wrote: "it has been entirely without solicitation on my part." [17] Eight years later he was again elected though he declared that he had "never attended a public meeting or been at the home of a single individual, and though my adversary and his friends had ransacked the county in the old Electioneering Style." [18]

The contrast between ideal and reality was well illustrated by statements made during an election quarrel in Accomac County. The following advice was given to the freeholders: "If a man sollicits you earnestly for your vote, avoid him; self-interest and sordid avarice lurk under his forced smiles, hearty shakes by the hand, and deceitfully enquires after your wife and family." However, it was said, referring to the candidates, that "every person who observes the two gentlemen, allows that the smiles of Mr. S—h are more forced than Mr. H—ry's, and of this Mr. S—h himself is so conscious that he has declared, he would give an Hundred Pounds could he shake hands with the freeholders, and smile in their faces with as good a grace as Col. Pa—e, that he might be more equally match'd." [19]

Some candidates sought to injure a rival by starting the rumor that he was withdrawing from the race,[20] that he had joined interests with an unpopular man, that he was a common drunkard, that he despised poor folks, or that "It's his doings our levies are so high." [21] If the rumor was false, it was better for the candidate to keep silent and let one of his supporters circulate it. More often, the candidate, with the help of his friends, undertook to set himself and his views on current issues in a favorable light.

Sir John Toddy, whose supporters were great lovers of rum, promised to get the price of that article reduced,[22] and it is said of Strutabout that "he'll promise to move mountains. He'll make the rivers navigable, and bring the tide over the tops of the hills, for a vote." [23] The noble Worthy promised no more than to "endeavour faithfully to discharge the trust you have reposed in me." [24] And Wou'dbe answered the questions of the voters with carefully measured words. When asked if he would reduce the price of rum and remove an unpopular tax, he answered, "I could not," explaining that it would be beyond his power to accomplish these things. His position on other matters is set forth in the following dialogue.

Stern. Suppose, Mr. Wou'dbe, we that live over the river, should want to come to church on this side, is it not very hard we should pay ferryage; when we pay as much to the church as you do?

Wou'dbe. Very hard.

Stern. Suppose we were to petition the assembly could you get us clear of that expense?

Wou'dbe. I believe it to be just; and make no doubt but it would pass into a law.

Stern. Will you do it?

Wou'dbe. I will endeavour to do it.

Stern. Huzza for Mr. Wou'dbe! Wou'dbe forever!

Prize. Why don't you burgesses, do something with the damn'd pickers? If we have a hogshead of tobacco refused, away it goes to them; and after they have twisted up the best of it for their own use, and taken as much as will pay them for their trouble, the poor planter has little for his share.

Wou'dbe. There are great complaints against them; and I believe the assembly will take them under consideration.

Prize. Will you vote against them?

Wou'dbe. I will, if they deserve it.[25]

Littlepage, it will be recalled, promised to fight the existing system of tobacco inspection, and thereby was said to have gained much favor with the people. He also proposed to have the inspectors chosen yearly by the freeholders of the county, an extension of democracy which must have seemed radical to some men of the time.[26] Friends of George Wythe, appealing to those who felt burdened by taxes, declared that "he would serve as Burgess for the said County for nothing," and they offered to "give Bond to repay any Thing that should be levied on the County for him." A rival candidate, William Wager, realizing that he must follow suit, immediately upon "hearing this Declaration, came up and said, he would serve on the same terms." [27]

There is some evidence that the House of Burgesses frowned upon campaign commitments by candidates, especially upon those which reflected upon the prerogative of the House by promising that it would act according to the will of a single member. The powerful Committee of Privileges and Elections investigated the making of campaign promises by some of the candidates, and the committee gave detailed reports to the House of its findings. Perhaps it was to protect himself against the disapproval of the House that Littlepage, who had promised much during his campaign, "Just before the Poll was opened...publickly and openly declared, in the Court House, before a great Number of People, that he did not look upon any of the Promises he had made to the People as binding on him, but that they were all void." [28]

There is no way of knowing how many of the candidates followed the rule approved by the Carters, Tucker, and Munford's character Wou'dbe: "never to ask a vote for myself," [29] and how many of them followed the example of Littlepage in unashamedly and energetically courting the voters wherever they could find them, even going on house-to-house canvasses. Most of the candidates seem to have operated between these extremes. While they did not insulate themselves from the voters before elections, they avoided unseemly and ostentatious activity in their mingling with the people. The distinction between approved and disapproved conduct was close, and it is easier to be sure that a line was drawn than to be sure just where it was drawn. A man was likely to shift it a bit, depending on whether he was judging his own actions or those of his rival. John Clopton once gave his candidate son shrewd advice about cultivating the people and tricking a rival at the very time that he was fulminating against the tricks, deceptions, and intimidations practiced by the son's opponents! [30]

Whether the candidates actively campaigned or not, a good many votes were committed before the election. The Quakers or the Presbyterians, the men along the south side of a river or in the northern corner of a county—these and other groups might discuss the candidates and decide which of them to support. Similarly, powerful men would let their friends, relatives, and dependents know how they stood toward the candidates. Thus, elections were often settled before they were held. A curious attempt to hold back this natural operation of democracy was made in a brief notice published in the *Virginia Gazette*. It was addressed "To the free and independent ELECTORS of the borough of NORFOLK," and it desired them "not to engage your votes or interest until the day of election, as a Gentleman of undoubted ability intends to declare himself as a candidate on that day, and hopes to succeed." [31]

From these cases it is evident that although many candidates entered the race several weeks before election day, a few of them, like the unnamed gentleman of Norfolk or like Worthy in Munford's play, waited until the last minute before announcing their decision to stand a poll. John Marshall recalled in his old age that he had had the unusual experience of being made a candidate contrary to his wishes. He described the event, which occurred at Richmond during an election to the Virginia legislature in the spring of 1795, in the following words.

"I attended at the polls to give my vote early & return to the court which was then in session at the other end of the town. As soon as the election commenced a gentleman came forward and demanded that a poll should be taken for me. I was a good deal surprized at this entirely unexpected proposition & declared my decided dissent. I said that if my fellow citizens wished it I would become a candidate at the next succeeding election, but that I could not consent to serve this year because my wishes & my honour were engaged for one of the candidates. I then voted for my friend & left the polls for the court which was open and waiting for me. The gentleman said that he had a right to demand a poll for whom he pleased, & persisted in his demand that one should be opened for me—I might if elected refuse to obey the voice of my constituents if I chose to do so. He then gave his vote for me.

"As this was entirely unexpected—not even known to my brother who though of the same political opinions with myself was the active & leading partisan of the candidate against whom I voted, the election was almost suspended for ten or twelve minutes, and a consultation took place among the principal freeholders. They then came in and in the evening information was brought me that I was elected. I regretted this for the sake of my friend. In other respects I was well satisfied at being again in the assembly." [32]

Many of the candidates may have been perfectly circumspect in their pre-election behavior, but all of them, with hardly an exception, relied on the persuasive powers of food and drink dispensed to the voters with open-handed liberality. Theoderick Bland, Jr., once wrote with apparent scorn that "Our friend, Mr. Banister, has been very much ingaged ever since the dissolution of the assembly, in swilling the planters with bumbo." [33] When he supplied the voters with liquor Banister was in good company; it included Washington, Jefferson, and John Marshall. [34]

The favorite beverage was rum punch. Cookies and ginger cakes were often provided, and occasionally there was a barbecued bullock and several hogs. The most munificent as well as democratic kind of treat was a public occasion, a sort of picnic, to which the freeholders in general were invited. [35] George Washington paid the bills for another kind of treat in connection with his Fairfax County campaigns for a seat in the House of Burgesses. It consisted of a supper and ball on the night of the election, replete with fiddler, "Sundries &ca." On at least one occasion he shared the cost of the ball with one or more persons, perhaps with the other successful candidate, for his memorandum of expenses closes with the words: "By Cash paid Captn. Dalton for my part of ye Expense at the Election Ball. £ 8. 5. 6." [36]

A supper and ball of this kind was probably more exclusive than a picnic-type of treat. Hospitality was often shown also to small groups, usually composed of important and influential men. Munford describes a breakfast given the morning of the election by Wou'dbe for the principal freeholders. Worthy was the guest of honor; fine salt shad, warm toast and butter, coffee, tea, or chocolate, with spirits for lacing the chocolate, were set before the guests; and although it was said that "we shall have no polling now," it was understood that all were for Worthy and Wou'dbe.[37]

It was a common practice for candidates to keep open house for the freeholders on their way to the election, and it is a marvel where space was found for all to sleep. When Little-page heard that some of the voters who lived more than twenty-five miles from the courthouse were unwilling to ride so far in cold weather, he invited them to call at his house which was about five miles from the courthouse. Some ten of them came and were hospitably entertained, "though their Entertainment was not more than was usual with him." Some of the company "were pretty merry with Liquor when they came" to his home. That evening "they chiefly drank Cider." "Some of them drank Drams in the Morning, and went merry to the Court House."[38]

Candidates frequently arranged for treats to be given in their names by someone else. Lieutenant Charles Smith managed this business for George Washington during a campaign in Frederick County in 1758. Two days after the election, which Washington had not been able to attend, Smith sent him receipts for itemized accounts that he had paid to five persons who had supplied refreshments for the voters.[39] A year or two earlier in Elizabeth City County Thomas Craghead sought to repay William Wager, a candidate for burgess, for help he had once received in time of distress. He invited several people to Wager's house and out of his own purse entertained them with "Victuals and Drink." He also had a share in treating all who were present at a muster of Captain Wager's militia company, after which they drank Wager's health.[40]

Samuel Overton, a candidate in Hanover County, directed Jacob Hundley "to prepare a Treat for some of the Freeholders of the said County at his House." Later, Overton withdrew from the race, but a group of freeholders, perhaps ignorant of Overton's withdrawal, came to Hundley's house. He thereupon sent a messenger, desiring Overton's "Directions whether they were to be treated at his Expense," and Overton ordered him "to let them have four Gallons of Rum made into punch, and he would pay for it."

At this juncture some of the finer points of campaigning begin to appear. Littlepage, an active candidate, was among those present at Hundley's house; and Littlepage had agreed in return for Overton's withdrawal to reimburse Overton the sum of £75, which was the expense he had incurred in this and a previous election. As a codicil it was agreed that Littlepage would pay only £50 in case "Mr. Henry," presumably Patrick Henry, should enter the race and be elected. While the treat was in progress Hundley told Littlepage "that the Liquor was all drank." He immediately ordered two gallons more, telling Hundley that he supposed Overton would pay for it. Whether any of the company heard this conversation is in doubt; but this much is clear, that Littlepage paid Overton to withdraw, that Littlepage attended a treat for Overton's friends, and that Littlepage succeeded, according to the testimony of one of the guests, in winning "the Interest" of most of them.[41]

On election day the flow of liquor reached high tide. Douglas S. Freeman calculated that during a July election day in Frederick County in the year 1758, George Washington's agent supplied 160 gallons to 391 voters and "unnumbered hangers-on." This amounted to more than a quart and a half a voter. An itemized list of the refreshments included 28 gallons of rum, 50 gallons of rum punch, 34 gallons of wine, 46 gallons of beer, and 2 gallons of cider royal.[42] During the close and bitter struggle between John Marshall and John Clopton for a seat in Congress in 1799, a "barrel of whiskey . . . with the head knocked in" was on the courthouse green.[43]

Defeated candidates often complained of the wrongdoing of their successful opponents. George Douglas of Accomac County alleged before the Committee of Privileges and Elections that Edmund Scarburgh, shortly before the issuance of the writ of election, had twice given "strong Liquors to the People of the said County; once at a Race, and the other Time at a Muster; and did, on the Day of Election, cause strong Liquor to be brought in a Cart, near the Court-house Door, where many People drank thereof, whilst the Polls of the Election were taking; and one Man in particular, said, *Give me a Drink, and I will go and vote for Col.* Scarburgh, . . . and drink was accordingly given him out of the said Cart, where several People were merry with Drink: But it doth not appear, whether that Person voted for the said *Scarburgh,* or not; or was a Freeholder." Contrary to the recommendation of the Committee, Scarburgh was seated.[44]

Captain Robert Bernard was charged with intimidation as well as improper treating in his efforts to help Beverley Whiting win an election in Gloucester County. He attended a private muster of Captain Hayes' men and solicited the freeholders among them to vote for Whiting. "And the next Day, at a Muster of his own Company, the said *Bernard* brought

40 Gallons of Cyder, and 20 Gallons of Punch into the Field, and treated his Men, solliciting them to vote for Mr. *Whiting,* as they came into the Field; and promised one *James Conquest,* to give him Liquor, if he would vote for Mr. *Whiting,* which *Conquest* refused; and then *Bernard* said he should be welcome to drink, tho' he would not vote for him: That the said *Bernard* promised one *Gale,* a Freeholder to pay his Fine, if he would stay from the Election; which *Gale* accordingly did: That the Day of Election, the said *Bernard* treated several Freeholders, who said they would vote for Mr. *Whiting,* at one *Sewell's* Ordinary: And that, at the Election, one of the Freeholders said, he was going to vote for Mr. *Whiting,* because he had promised Capt. *Bernard* so to do; but that he had rather give Half a Pistole than do it: And other Freeholders, who were indebted to Col. *Whiting,* said, that Capt. *Bernard* told them, that Col. *Whiting* would be angry with them if they voted against Mr. *Whiting;* which the said *Bernard* denied, upon his Oath, before the Committee."

The House of Burgesses compelled Bernard to acknowledge his offense, to ask the pardon of the House, and to pay certain fees; and it requested the Governor to issue a writ for a new election in Gloucester County.[45]

The law strictly prohibited any person "directly or indirectly" from giving "money, meat, drink, present, gift, reward, or entertainment...in order to be elected, or for being elected to serve in the General Assembly";[46] but in one way or another nearly all the candidates gave treats, and seldom was a voice raised in protest. One of the rare protests was adopted at a general meeting of the citizens of Williamsburg two years before the Declaration of Independence. In an address to Peyton Randolph, who was a candidate for reelection to the House of Burgesses, the townsmen declared themselves to be "greatly scandalized at the Practice which has too much prevailed throughout the Country of entertaining the Electors, a Practice which even its Antiquity cannot sanctify; and being desirous of setting a worthy Example to our Fellow Subjects, in general, for abolishing every Appearance of Venality (that only Poison which can infect our happy Constitution) and to give the fullest Proof that it is to your singular Merit alone you are indebted for the unbought Suffrages of a free People; moved, Sir, by these important Considerations, we earnestly request that you will not think of incurring any Expense or Trouble at the approaching Election of a Citizen, but that you will do us the Honour to partake of an Entertainment which we shall direct to be provided for the Occasion." [47]

Three years later young James Madison, feeling that "the corrupting influence of spiritous liquors, and other treats," was "inconsistent with the purity of moral and republican principles," and wishing to see the adoption of "a more chaste mode of conducting elections in Virginia," determined "by an example, to introduce it." He found, however, that voters preferred free rum to the high ideals of a young reformer; "that the old habits were too deeply rooted to be suddenly reformed." He was defeated by rivals who did not scruple to use "all the means of influence familiar to the people." [48] For many years to come liquor had a large part in Virginia elections. In 1795 Jefferson wrote that he was in despair because "the low practices" of a candidate in Albemarle County were "but too successful with the unthinking who merchandize their votes for grog." [49] In 1807 Nathaniel Beverley Tucker, writing from Charlotte Court House, informed his father, St. George Tucker, that "In this part of the state ... every decent man is striving to get a seat in the legislature. There are violent contests every where that I have been, to the great anoyance of old John Barleycorn, who suffers greatly in the fray." [50]

Although the custom of treating was deeply ingrained, the law was not entirely disregarded. It did not prohibit a man's offering refreshment to a friend; it only prohibited treating "in order to be elected." Through various interpretations of these words most of the candidates found ways of dispensing largess to the freeholders without incurring the censure of the House of Burgesses and perhaps without suffering from an uneasy conscience. Everyone would agree that it was wrong to give liquor to "one *Grubbs*, a Freeholder," who announced at an election that "he was ready to vote for any one who would give him a Dram." [51] Neither should a candidate ask votes of those whom he was entertaining though it was perhaps all right for him to make the general remark "that if his Friends would stand by him he should carry his Election." [52] Some men thought that there should be no treating after the election writ was issued until the poll had been taken. James Littlepage "expressly ordered" Paul Tilman, whom he had employed "to prepare his Entertainment at the Election ... not to give the Freeholders any Liquor until after the closing of the Poll," and Littlepage produced evidence to show that "none of them had any Liquor, except some few who insisted on it, and paid for it themselves." [53]

To avoid the appearance of corruption, it was well for the candidate to have the reputation of being hospitable at all times. When William Wager's campaign was under investigation, especially in the matter of the treat given in his home by one of his friends and another treat given in his honor to his militia company, Wager introduced evidence to show that he customarily entertained all who came to his house, strangers as well as freeholders, and that he usually treated the members of his militia company with punch after the exercises were over. "They would after that come before his Door and fire Guns in Token of their Gratitude, and then he would give them Punch 'til they dispersed, and that this had been a frequent Practice for several Years." [54]

To avoid the reality as well as the appearance of corruption, the candidates usually made a point of having it understood that the refreshments were equally free to men of every political opinion. If a candidate's campaign was under investigation, it was much in his favor if he could show that among his guests were some who had clearly said that they did not intend to vote for him.[55] Washington reflected an acceptable attitude when he wrote while arranging for the payment of large bills for liquor consumed during a Frederick County election: "I hope no Exception were taken to any that voted against me but that all were alike treated and all had enough; it is what I much desir'd." [56] Washington seems to have followed this policy in subsequent elections. A young Englishman, who witnessed an election at Alexandria in 1774 when Washington was one of the two successful candidates, wrote: "The Candidates gave the populace a Hogshead of Toddy (what we call Punch in England). In the evening the returned Member gave a Ball to the Freeholders and Gentlemen of the town. This was conducted with great harmony. Coffee and Chocolate, but no Tea. This Herb is in disgrace among them at present." [57]

Bountiful supplies of free liquor were responsible for much

rowdiness, fighting, and drunkenness, but the fun and excitement of an election and the prospect of plentiful refreshments of the kind customarily consumed in that day helped to bring the voters to the polls. Thus in a perverse kind of way treating made something of a contribution to eighteenth-century democracy. Although one sometimes found a man who lived by the rule, "never to taste of a man's liquor unless I'm his friend," [58] most of the voters accepted such refreshments as were offered. As they drank, they were less likely to feel that they were incurring obligations than that the candidate was fulfilling his obligation. According to the thinking of that day, the candidate ought to provide refreshments for the freeholders. His failure to fulfill this obligation would be interpreted as a sign of "pride or parsimony," as a "want of respect" for the voters, as James Madison found to his sorrow.[59]

The Virginia voter expected the candidate to be manly and forthright, but he wanted the candidate to treat him with due respect. He had the power to approve and reject, and the sum total of this consciousness of power among the voters was a strong and significant aspect of the democratic spirit in eighteenth-century Virginia.

CHAPTER FIVE

Gentlemen of

Long-Tailed Families

THE READINESS with which the eighteenth-century Virginian came to elections, the efforts of the candidates to win his support, and his assumption that they owed him plentiful quantities of rum punch suggest that the freeholders had a large measure of political power which they freely exercised. Political power truly rested in the people; democracy was a real and active force. At the same time a large measure of political power was vested in the few; aristocracy was also a strong and positive force in politics. Eighteenth-century Virginia did not regard democracy and aristocracy as contradictory kinds of government. It employed both of these qualities in its political system, and it was the interplay of these two forces, democratic and aristocratic, that gave to the government of colonial Virginia much of that distinctive quality which made for the selection of those men who ruled Virginia during the era of the American Revolution.

Colonial Virginians, with their British background of a class society and with obvious differences in wealth and social position on every hand in Virginia, accepted the inequality of man as a fact. The Reverend James Maury, principal in the Parsons' case, once put the matter very bluntly by contrasting "gentlemen" on the one hand with the members of "the vulgar herd" on the other.[1] Although Maury's distinction was too sharp and his language too harsh for some of his contemporaries, most of them would have agreed that society was composed of several levels which were "separated by no marked lines, but shading off imperceptibly from top to bottom." At the top were the "aristocrats, composed of the great landholders who had seated themselves below tide water on the main rivers, and lived in a style of luxury and extravagance, insupportable by the other inhabitants, and which, indeed, ended, in several instances, in the ruin of their own fortunes." Next were "the younger sons and daughters of the aristocrats, who inherited the pride of their ancestors, without their wealth. Then came the pretenders, men who from vanity, or the impulse of growing wealth, or from that enterprize which is natural to talents, sought to detach themselves from the plebeian ranks, to which they properly belonged, and imitated, at some distance, the manners and habits of the great. Next to these, were a solid and independent yeomanry, looking askance at those above, yet not venturing to jostle them." [2]

The term "gentry" was usually applied to the upper segment of society, and the individual men of the class were spoken of as "gentlemen." The eighteenth-century Virginian could recognize a gentleman by his name, his manners, and his dress, by the wig that he wore and the carriage that he provided for his family. In religion he was likely to be an Episcopalian; often he was a vestryman. His house was large, his lands extensive, and his slaves numerous. Shunning solitude, he sought pleasure in the chase and horse-racing, gaming and heavy drinking. He was "open-handed and open-hearted;

fond of society, indulging in all its pleasures, and practising all its courtesies. But these social virtues also occasionally ran into the kindred vices of love of show, haughtiness, sensuality." [3]

Although many of the gentry were educated, few had the scholarly instincts and thoughtfulness of Madison and Jefferson. But learning was respected by many of those who wanted no part of it for themselves. Philip Fithian, after spending a year as tutor in Virginia, came to the conclusion that Virginians rated men largely in terms of wealth, "excepting always the value they put upon posts of honour, & mental acquirements." To illustrate his point he observed that a Princeton graduate "would be rated, without any more questions asked, either about your family, your Estate, your business, or your intention, at 10,000 £; and you might come, & go, & converse, & keep company, according to this value; and you would be dispised & slighted if yo[u] rated yourself a farthing cheaper." [4]

Respect for the educated man was not limited to the gentry. Philip Mazzei, friend and neighbor of Jefferson, when speaking of "those who work in the fields, or who practice some mechanical trade," observed that "Those with only a limited education have great respect for persons who have had more than they. They take it for granted, whenever in doubt, especially in matters pertaining to the public weal, that they have a right to consult a person with a better education." [5] Munford's freeholders speak with approval of a candidate because he was "a man of sense, and had larning." [6]

A Virginia gentleman could also be recognized by the offices that he held, for office, except such lowly posts as constable, was a prerogative of men of property and family. The law required no more property of the officeholder than it did of the voter, but custom and public opinion were more demanding. Jefferson once objected to the office of county lieutenant being given to a man "not possessing an inch of property in the county or other means of obtaining influence over the people, and of a temper so ungovernable that instead of reconciling he will by his manner of executing revolt the minds of the people against the calls of government." [7] Governor Dinwiddie sent a scathing letter to an official who had bestowed a colonelcy on a man who "has no Estate in the County, and keeps an Ordinary," and a captaincy on "a Person insolvent and not able to pay his Levy. . . . This Conduct is prostituting my Commissions entrusted with You, and pray what Gentlemen of Character will role with such Persons that have neither Land nor Negroes, at same time of very bad Characters, having no just Caling to maintain themselves, and in Course makes great Distractions in the County? Your Family and Property engaged Me to confide in You, but I am sorry that I am obliged to say Your Conduct is much contrary to my Expectations, and, indeed, to that of a Gentleman of Your Family and Estate." [8] Despite his insistence that only gentlemen should hold office, Dinwiddie found himself displeased with some of the gentlemen in office. He wrote of Lewis Burwell, one of the most powerful men in the colony: "He apprehends he is troubled with many distempers, and conceives he has a Cancer; but in fact it's a distemper in the Mind, [from] which I believe he will never recover." The Governor laid plans to clip his wings, laying his plans shrewdly and preparing to move cautiously because, as he expressed it, "he has a long tailed family." [9]

Membership in a prominent family and the possession of

a considerable estate did not, of course, necessarily place a man in office. But those in office so generally had these qualifications that lists of local and provincial officials constitute a convenient index to the names of the families that composed the gentry.

At the peak of the official hierarchy were the members of the council, who were chosen from the top families of the planter aristocracy. They held important and lucrative offices such as auditor general, receiver general, and secretary of the colony, and they were in a favorable position, which they did not hesitate to use, to secure large grants of land. Good family helped to put a man in the council; in turn, membership in the council enabled a man to improve the fortunes of his family. The advantages of this office were enjoyed by a rather small number of families interrelated by blood and marriage. One kind of relationship is indicated by the fact that only fifty-seven family names appear in a list of the ninety-one men appointed to the council from 1680 to the Revolution. Nine family names account for almost a third of the councilors during this century; and fourteen other names for almost another third. Five councilors bore the name of Page; three each the names of Burwell, Byrd, Carter, Custis, Harrison, Lee, Ludwell, and Wormley.[10]

The most numerous and widespread of the officeholders were the justices of the peace. A hundred years later this office had fallen into such disrepute that it could be spoken of in the following fashion by a judge of the Supreme Court of the State of Georgia.

"The law does not require a justice of the peace to charge the jury at all; his ignorance of the law, as well as propriety, would seem to demand that he should not, but if he undertakes to instruct the jury, he must do it correctly, and in accordance with law. A justice of the peace is generally a man of consequence in his neighborhood; he writes the wills draws the deeds and pulls the teeth of the people; also he performs divers surgical operations on the animals of his neighbors. The justice has played his part on the busy stage of life from the time of Mr. Justice Shallow down to the time of Mr. Justice Riggins. Who has not seen the gapping, listening crowd assembled around his honor, the justice, on tiptoe to catch the words of wisdom as they fell from his venerated lips?

> "And still they gazed
> And still the wonder grew
> That one small head
> Could carry all he knew." [11]

But in eighteenth-century Virginia the justiceship of the peace was an honorable and dignified office. "Gentleman" or "Esq." was usually written after the name of a justice; and the justices of a county were referred to collectively as "gentlemen justices." These were well chosen titles, for justices of the peace were generally members of the gentry. They were also men of much power in local affairs, for all of the justices were members of the county court, the governing body of the county.

In the last twenty years before the American Revolution some 1600 men were justices of the peace in Virginia. Four hundred and twenty of the 1600 belonged to one or another of fifty-five families, using the word family in its ample Virginia sense. No more than three or four hundred families supplied at least three fourths of the justices during the last twenty years of the colonial period.[12] These three or four hundred families—some of which like the Randolphs were clans spread widely over the colony—made up a large part of that segment of society known as the gentry.

The economic and social standing of the justices is indicated by the amount of property listed after their names on the tax books. Although the justices and their families constituted slightly less than 2 per cent of the white population in eight sample counties—Charles City, Northumberland, and Essex in the Tidewater, Albemarle, Orange, and Halifax in the Piedmont, and Rockbridge and Shenandoah west of the Blue Ridge—they paid 8.6 per cent of the total land tax in these counties and 12.4 per cent of the tax on slaves. Of horses, the justices owned 5.7 per cent, and 22.3 per cent of the carriages were theirs. Each justice, on an average, paid taxes on 903 acres of land, eight horses, and on thirteen slaves over twelve years old, indicating an average holding of about twenty-five slaves of all ages. And one justice in six or seven kept a carriage. All of these, especially land, slaves, and carriages, were measures of social position as well as of wealth.[13]

Carriages being unnecessary as well as expensive were acquired only by those of high social position or with aspirations in that direction. The plain farmer or the planter with a practical turn of mind was content to take his wife and children to church on horseback or in a wagon. The tax on carriages was in the nature of a luxury tax, and it was levied according to the number of wheels so that the four-wheeled coach bore twice the tax of the two-wheeled chaise. Only 394 wheels were listed for taxation in the eight counties being considered, and of these 88 belonged to justices of the peace. Most of the carriages listed for taxation were in the older tidewater counties. Only ten wheels were reported in Rockbridge and

Shenandoah counties, and six of these belonged to justices of the peace. In these two counties no man owned as many as twenty slaves of taxable age; for large slaveholdings, like carriages, were found mostly in the East. Of the six persons in Rockbridge and Shenandoah counties who owned ten or more taxable slaves, four were justices.

West of the Blue Ridge, the justices owned fewer slaves and carriages than those in the tidewater counties and, for that matter, paid smaller land taxes and owned fewer horses, but their position in their communities was no less high. They lived where there was less wealth, but of such as there was they had more than their share. Wherever they lived, whether in Tidewater, Piedmont, or west of the Blue Ridge, the justices ranked among the wealthiest men of their community.

The justices were near the top in wealth, but they did not compose all of the top.[14] In the year 1788 not over a third of the wealthiest men were justices. However, there were some like Jefferson and Washington who had once served on the bench but had retired from it under the pressure of other duties either public or private. The retirement of a man of wealth was often accompanied by the elevation of a younger relative who, in effect, represented wealth even though he had little property of his own. At one time or another perhaps half of the wealthiest men of eighteenth-century Virginia served as justices of the peace.

These men of wealth, social position, and great power in county government also had much influence in burgess elections and therefore in provincial government. Some of the ways in which they influenced burgess elections were apparent during the taking of a poll at Frederick Court House, now known as Winchester, on July 24, 1758. One of the candidates was Colonel George Washington. Three years earlier he had been defeated at this same place. Now his plans were well laid, and his prospects were favorable except for the fact that his military duties kept him at Fort Cumberland during the critical days before the election and on election day itself. To offset this disadvantage, Washington's friends rallied handsomely to his support, and Colonel James Wood, an influential man in Frederick County politics, agreed to sit in his place to thank those who voted for Washington.

There were four candidates for the two seats. Hugh West and Captain Thomas Swearingen were standing for reelection. Washington, who was twenty-six years old, was one of the two young men seeking to replace them. The other was Colonel Thomas Bryan Martin, nephew of Thomas Lord Fairfax, who had represented Hampshire County in the previous assembly.[15]

When sheriff, clerks, and candidates had taken their seats and all was in readiness for the election to begin, Lord Fairfax came before them. If any man in the county had a claim to first place, Fairfax was the man. He was proprietor of great landholdings in the region, he was county lieutenant and ranking magistrate of the Frederick County Court, and he had the unique distinction of having been especially commissioned to act as a justice of the peace in all of the counties of the Northern Neck.[16] Fairfax began the election by voting for Martin and Washington. At his heels was William Meldrum, an Episcopal clergyman and the chief ecclesiastic of the region,[17] who also supported Washington and Martin. The third voter was Washington's representative, Colonel James Wood. Naturally, he voted for Washington, but for West instead of for Martin. The fourth was also a colonel, John Carlyle, whose votes were given for Martin and Washington.

These first four votes, given by leaders of the landed gentry and of political, military and ecclesiastical institutions, set the pattern for the rest of the election. Nearly every man who can be identified on the poll sheets as a man of rank and position was for Washington and Martin. In addition to Lord Fairfax there was Fielding Lewis, Esq., and four persons designated as "Gentleman." All six of these voted for Washington and Martin. So did the sole physician, Doctor James Craik, and the three ministers, one a Presbyterian, another a Baptist, and the third the Reverend Mr. Meldrum. Eight voters, including George William Fairfax, bore the military titles of colonel, captain, or lieutenant. From these, Washington received seven votes, Martin six, and West three. Not a man from any of these groups of important persons voted for Swearingen.

Before fifty votes had been cast it was evident that Washington was leading, followed closely by Martin. Swearingen was trailing so far behind that it seemed useless to waste a vote on him. In the last half of the election he received practically none while West began to pull up toward Martin. Perhaps West's friends waited until the latter part of the election to vote, just as the friends of Martin and Washington did most of the voting in the early stages. Or it may be that those who disliked to follow the lead of the titled gentlemen concentrated on West when they saw that Swearingen had no chance. When all had voted and the polls were tallied, the candidates for whom Lord Fairfax had given the opening vote were found to be elected, the vote standing Washington 310, Martin 240, West 199, and Swearingen 45.[18]

Several legal devices enabled the man of wealth and social position to make his political influence felt. One device was the practice of oral voting. When Lord Fairfax, Colonel James Wood, and Colonel John Carlyle voted for a candidate at the beginning of the election, they turned to that candidate the votes of lesser men who respected their judgment or who were obligated to them. If a young man wished to rise in politics, society, or wealth, it was well for him to vote for those who had the power to aid him in winning his goal. A tavernkeeper, a blacksmith, or a cobbler would be tempted to vote as his wealthier patrons voted. The man in straitened circumstances would be inclined to support those to whom he was beholden or who might give him aid.

The political influence of the wealthy man was enhanced by the provision allowing him to vote in every county in which he could meet the freehold requirement. The wealthy man was eligible to vote in more counties than a yeoman farmer, and he could more readily spare the time to go from county court to county court when elections were being held.

The man with extensive landholdings could also weigh his chances in the various counties in which he owned land and stand a poll in the one which offered the brightest prospects. Law and custom permitted him to represent any county in which he was entitled to vote.[19] Some of the most distinguished Virginia statesmen advanced in office more rapidly because of this provision. George Washington, a resident of Fairfax County, was first elected to the House of Burgesses in Frederick County some fifty miles to the west. Patrick Henry, while living in Hanover County, began his legislative career when he was elected to represent Louisa County in May, 1765. In 1782 John Marshall was elected to the House from

Fauquier although he was spending part of his time in Richmond where he was soon to make his residence.[20] Benjamin Harrison, upon retiring from the governorship in 1784, sought to reenter the House of Delegates as a representative of Charles City County where he resided. But he, the father of one President of the United States and the grandfather of another, was defeated by John Tyler, the father of President John Tyler. Thereupon Harrison became a candidate in Surry County, won the election, entered the House, and defeated Tyler for the speakership.[21]

As members of the county court, the important men of the county wielded something of a corporate influence at election time. If an election turned into a sharp division between gentry and small farmers, the justices could muster a considerable block of votes from among themselves, their families, and the various officials of the court; and they could count on the votes of cautious freeholders who, remembering the great powers of the court, would hesitate to vote for a candidate who was clearly disapproved of by the justices.

One of the chief instruments of the court's political power was the sheriff. He was responsible for the management of elections, and he was, of course, expected to be impartial. He was not even allowed to vote in elections over which he presided except to break a tie.[22] Nevertheless, his power to influence the outcome of an election was considerable. He set the day for the election, often with an eye to whether this day or that would best suit the interests of the candidates he favored. He opened the poll when he pleased and closed it when he pleased, sometimes closing it despite the pleas of a candidate to keep the poll open until more voters could be corralled. It was his right to decide whether individual voters were properly qualified.[23] Even when the sheriff presided over the election with utmost decorum and fairness, each voter standing before the sheriff to give publicly his vote was aware that he stood before a man of great power and importance. If the sheriff was known to favor one candidate over another, some voters may well have been swayed by this knowledge.

Thomas Marshall, father of the Chief Justice, once demonstrated in a fashion not above reproach one of the ways a sheriff could use his power to influence an election. In June, 1769, Marshall, while sheriff of Fauquier County, let it be known that he would be a candidate for burgess. He made this announcement some three months before the election was held and two months before the writ ordering the election was received. A sheriff could not be a burgess, but Marshall delayed resigning the shrievalty until he had received the writ, set the day for the election, and caused official notices to be read. Then he resigned. Marshall had shrewdly set the election on September 18, choosing that day because one of his rivals expected the support of twenty residents of neighboring Stafford County who were qualified to vote in Fauquier, and the Stafford election had been scheduled for September 18. The House of Burgesses later reprimanded Marshall for this action, but inasmuch as he was elected by so large a majority that "his Conduct had no Effect upon the Election for Fauquier," it seated him.[24]

As Marshall's case indicates, the sheriff could use his power for personal aggrandizement. More often, however, he served the general cause of the justices of the county or one of the factions in that group. The frequent rotation of the office of sheriff, in contrast to the long tenure customary in the county clerkship, prohibited the man who was sheriff from building up a position of personal political power independent of the county court which would endure over a span of years. The office of sheriff was usually held only for a year or two by any one man. It customarily went to the ranking justice of the county who had not previously held this office. When he came to office the sheriff had been a member of the county court for a long time, and naturally he usually represented the interest of the gentry when he managed burgess elections.

Some of the customs and attitudes of the times also operated to the advantage of the gentry in elections. The practice of treating the voters excluded a poor man from candidacy for the simple reason that he could not afford to buy meat and drink for the voters in the large quantities that were expected. Samuel Overton of Hanover County estimated that his expenses for two elections amounted to £75.[25] George Washington spent about £25 on each of two elections,[26] over £39 on another, and approximately £50 on a fourth.[27] These were large amounts for that day—several times more than enough to buy the house and land of the voter who barely met the minimum franchise requirements. The custom of giving expensive treats also implied that candidates were wealthy and that they lived with the open-handed, lavish generosity of gentlemen. If a poor man scraped up enough money to stand an election and attempted to treat the voters like a gentleman, his performance was more likely to excite ridicule or pity than respect.

Like the custom of treating, the convention that candidates must not solicit votes for themselves operated in favor of the privileged class. Gentlemen could profit by the existence of the rule even though they did not always follow it. By frowning on house-to-house canvassing and other forms of personal solicitation of votes, they were, in effect, frowning on candidates who lacked the self-respect, the dignity, and some of the political advantages of the gentry. Gentlemen, let it plainly be said, wanted office despite their hostility to aggressive electioneering. But gentlemen knew how to seek support with such delicacy of phrase as to avoid the appearance of doing so, as did Colonel Richard Bland in the following note to Theoderick Bland, Sr.:

"Our election is to be on Thursday, the 27, of this month, which is this day week. I shall be glad to see you at it, . . . I hope I have given no occasion to the county, to refuse me at this time, and I shall always act to the utmost of my capacity, for the good of my electors, whose interest and my own, in great measure, are inseparable." [28]

The gentleman-candidate, knowing the leading men of the countryside, could ask their advice about standing for office and in the course of the conversation learn what support or "interests" he could count on. Asking for a man's support was more respectable than asking for a man's vote; and it was more rewarding. Thus the convention against personal canvassing among the voters worked to the advantage of gentlemen. So long as it could be maintained against the tendency of anxious candidates to breach it, Virginia was likely to fill its elective offices with members of the gentry.

The code of the gentleman was also apparent in certain customs in voting. Candidates did not vote for themselves in eighteenth-century Virginia, even in the midst of hard-fought, close elections. Early in the next century Henry St. George Tucker wrote: "That scoundrel Bailey was one of the Candidates. He got five blackguards to vote for him & concluded by voting for himself! He is a perfect unique." [29] But in the days of Washington and Jefferson, candidates either abstained from voting or voted for their opponents, and local custom determined which they did. In Northumberland elections of July 16, 1765, and July 25, 1771, and a Frederick election of July 24, 1758, none of the candidates voted. In Buckingham, Spotsylvania, Essex, and Westmoreland, they voted usually at the end of the election; but they did not vote for themselves.[30] For all their punctilio, gentlemen-candidates did not forget political shrewdness. A candidate would naturally vote for the man with whom he had joined interests. His other vote was usually for a man who was clearly elected or certainly defeated; not for a rival who might be put ahead by one or two more votes.[31]

The gentry had great influence in burgess elections, but they did not have absolute and unchallenged power to choose the county's representatives. Always they had to remember that freeholders were numerous enough to turn an election against an unpopular candidate even though he was supported by all the political weapons in the gentry's arsenal. In a Fairfax election of 1755 the gentry carried the day by the narrowest of margins. William Ellzey with the support of only one justice polled 220 votes, only two below George William Fairfax for whom eleven justices voted and twelve below John West who was supported by ten justices. There is at least a hint that the gentry was discomfited when James Littlepage defeated Nathaniel West Dandridge in Hanover County in 1764.[32]

In Northumberland County there was a contest that lasted for some years between the justices and a group that opposed them. In 1758 Colonel Presly Thornton, whose position is indicated by his title and his elevation in 1761 to the provincial Council, and Colonel Ball, sometime sheriff of Northumberland, overwhelmingly defeated "Mr. Robert Clarke,"[33] who was never a justice. The magistrates won handsomely, but they had taken no chances. All of them attended the election, and they gave eleven votes to Thornton and Ball and none to Clarke. The freeholders realized that much was at stake, for at least 329 of them voted in this election. Seven years later another election followed the same course; two candidates with the unanimous support of the justices were elected. However, the third candidate polled a larger vote than Clarke had polled.[34] Again, on July 25, 1771, Peter Presly Thornton, a Northumberland justice, defeated Thomas Downing, who was not a justice, in a single-member election. Here the margin was very close, with a difference of only two votes out of a total of 296 cast. But in this election the justices were not unanimously behind one of the candidates; two of the seventeen justices voting supported Downing.[35]

The justices ran much risk in supporting candidates who were not generally popular; democracy was strong enough to moderate autocratic tendencies in the gentry. In most elections, however, there is no evidence of tension between the justices and an opposition faction; the votes of the justices were usually divided among all of the candidates. The result in general was the election of burgesses who were more or less acceptable both to the leaders and to the rank and file of the voters.

Whether supported by the justices or not, the candidates for the House of Burgesses were almost without exception members of the gentry. Even Ellzey, who was opposed by nearly all of the justices of Fairfax County in 1755, was a ranking member of the county court just as West and Fairfax were. Swearingen, who received no support from men who can be recognized as members of the gentry of Frederick County in 1758, was a member of the court and a former representative of that county in the House of Burgesses.[36]

The truth of the matter is that the roster of eighteenth-century gentlemen served almost like a permanent list of nominees for political office. The function of the gentry was to provide candidates and often a measure of guidance as to which of these candidates to elect. The function of the rank and file of the freeholders was to decide which of the several gentlemen to send to the House of Burgesses and in the process to act as a check on any autocratic tendencies in the gentry. It was the interplay of these two forces, aristocratic and democratic, that produced the political leadership of revolutionary Virginia.

CHAPTER SIX

County Oligarchies

BIRTH INTO ONE of the ruling families was almost essential to the making of a political career in eighteenth-century Virginia. A man inherited local prominence from his father or uncle in much the same way that he inherited land and slaves and social position. It is difficult to recall the name of any Virginian of the Revolutionary generation who rose to high office without the aid of influential relatives. So it was with the Randolphs, Carters, Lees, Harrisons, and Nelsons; and so it was with men like Jefferson and Henry who are now known chiefly as revolutionists or as apostles of democracy. Thomas Jefferson's grandfather, who bore the same name, was a "gentleman justice" of Henrico County, a militia captain, and a sheriff.[1] Peter Jefferson, father of the author of the Declaration of Independence, held the offices of justice, sheriff, surveyor, and county lieutenant, and he was a member of the House of Burgesses and a vestryman of the parish of St. James, Northam.[2] Patrick Henry, another revolutionist and democrat, who, rightly or not, is often regarded as being more radical than Jefferson, was also born into a family of local prominence. His father was the presiding justice of the Hanover County Court, a militia colonel, and a vestryman, and his uncle was a clergyman of the Established Church.[3] Thus, when Jefferson and Henry began their political careers,

they were following in the footsteps of their fathers and kins-
men.

One can select at random from the prominent names of this
generation and discover that in nearly every case the man rose
to power on the shoulders of his father. James Madison's
father was a justice, a county lieutenant, and a vestryman.[4]
George Wythe's father was a member of the House of Burgesses.[5] George Washington's father, grandfather, and great
grandfather were justices of the peace. His father also held
the offices of churchwarden and sheriff,[6] and his half-brother
Lawrence of Mount Vernon was a burgess from Fairfax
County and a trustee of Alexandria.[7] The father of John
Marshall was the principal vestryman of Leeds parish as well
as justice of the peace, sheriff, and representative of Fauquier
County in the House of Burgesses.[8] Not his father but his
uncle Joseph Jones, who held many important offices in
colonial and revolutionary Virginia, aided James Monroe in
his political beginnings.[9]

Marriage into an influential family was also a distinct
asset in politics. Thomas Jefferson's father improved his
position by marrying Jane Randolph, a daughter of one of the
largest and most powerful families in Virginia. John Marshall's marriage to Mary Willis Ambler, daughter of Jacquelin Ambler, brought him influential connections. There
were, of course, other ways for a young man to gain the
attention and approval of older and more powerful men besides kinship and marriage. The early and close association
of George Washington with the Fairfaxes, especially with
Colonel William Fairfax, was an important element in the
beginning of his political career. This political alliance began
with Washington's supporting a son of Colonel Fairfax in an

election held just three years before Lord Fairfax led the procession of voters to the poll that sent Washington to the House of Burgesses for the first time.

Whether won through birth, marriage, or friendship, support from the gentry was indispensable for the man who would rise in politics in eighteenth-century Virginia. With enough men of the gentry on his side, a candidate was almost unbeatable. Munford's Wou'dbe, undisturbed by the report that "Strutabout and Smallhopes fawn and cringe in so abject a manner, for the few votes they get," was certain of victory, for he had "felt the pulse of all the leading men, and find they beat still for Worthy, and myself." [10]

Securely in the gentry through birth, marriage, and friendships, the ambitious young man usually made one or another of several local offices his next step in his political career. Election to the parish vestry, appointment to a militia office, or inclusion in the commission of the peace were all worthy aims for the man with political ambitions, but the most important of these was a justiceship of the peace.

The official duties of the justice were two-fold. Individually he had minor powers and responsibilities which included settling suits for small debts, issuing peace bonds, and ordering persons to appear before the county court to answer an indictment. Collectively the justices of a county constituted the county court. It was in this capacity that the justices made their major contribution to local affairs and received their major training in the art of government. [11]

In the colonial period and for many years thereafter, a man became a justice of the peace by qualifying under a commission issued by the governor. As the number of justices in a county was reduced by death, resignation, or removal, the governor in time issued a new commission for the county renaming those justices who continued to be active and adding new men to the court. Such an occasion allowed the governor to collect additional fees and offered him the opportunity to omit the name or to reduce to a lower place in the list any justice who had offended him. The justices strongly opposed the governor whenever he attempted to take advantage of this opportunity to make their tenure subject to his will.[12]

Through the vigor and effectiveness of their opposition to the governor, the Virginia justices established the point that for all practical purposes they could hold office for life. The personnel of the courts therefore changed but slowly; many a man served for twenty or thirty years. Out of the 1600 persons who served at one time or another as justices during the last score of years before the American Revolution, some 1200 of them were still on the bench when the last lists were made in this period.

The justices also established the practice of having the governor make additions to the court only on the recommendation of those who were already on the court. In line with this custom, the Essex County Court, at its February term in 1777, ordered that the names of seven men be transmitted "to his Excellency the Governor as Proper Persons to be commissioned as Justices: [in place of] Robert Beverley refusing to qualify, Meriwether Smith being one of the Council, William Woddrop going out of the Country, Augustine Moore being dead, and Thomas Waring in the Army to the northward, to be discontinued." [13]

The governor was not bound by law to accept the court's nomination, but because the court ordinarily consisted of the leading men of the county, men whose support he would wish to retain, he was usually disposed to follow their advice. If he did not, the previous members of the court might refuse to continue in office and thus virtually bring local government to a standstill. So it was in Spotsylvania County on June 5, 1744, when "Wm Johnston Gent, being asked whether he would accept & swear to the Commission of the Peace; now Produced, Answered, That he would not Accept and Swear to the Sd: Commission because Anthony Strother, William Hunter and William Lyne are put in the Commission without a Recommendation from the Court." Six other of the gentlemen justices followed the course taken by William Johnston, one of them observing that he refused "by reason he believes Doctor Wm Lyne has begged himself into the Comm: being not Recommended by the Court, which he takes to be slighting the Court." [14]

By such means as this the legal power of the governor to choose and commission justices was reduced to such an extent that he did little more than give formal approval to the wishes of the courts. Ordinarily the justices were not disposed to antagonize the governor, for he and his Council could be helpful to petitioners for land and other favors. But when the issue was drawn between the king's representative and colonial interests, the governor found himself unable to bend the county courts to his will or to use his appointive power to create a court party over the land. Long before the American Revolution the county courts had become, for all practical purposes, independent, self-perpetuating bodies, beyond the control of the governor or of any other branch of provincial government. Neither Williamsburg nor London controlled the government of the Virginia counties.

For that matter, the inhabitants of the county had no effec-

tive control over their court. Should it cease to function for
months or even years, should a bitter and prolonged quarrel
break out among the justices and destroy the usefulness of
the court, the inhabitants of the county could not vote them
out of office and replace them with more acceptable men.[15]
They might, of course, complain to the governor of the
"Illegal, Arbitrary, Partial and unjust proceedings" of the
justices,[16] but the people themselves had no legal process for
redressing their grievance. The justices would naturally feel
the pressure of public opinion in their county just as they
were subject to pressure by the great men in Williamsburg;
but in the last analysis, the county court could not be compelled to act contrary to its own will either by those beneath
it or by those above it.

Directly or indirectly, the court chose every other county
official. Some, such as the clerk, it elected outright; others,
namely the sheriff, the coroner, militia officers below the rank
of brigadier, and tobacco inspectors, were commissioned by the
governor on recommendation of the court.[17] Sometimes the
retiring official had much influence over the choice of his
successor. At the February term of the Essex County Court
in 1777, Hancock Lee was "appointed Clerk of this court in
the room of John Lee Gent. who resigned in his favour," [18]
and the Governor in Council was once informed that Spencer
Mottrom Ball of Northumberland County "resigns his right
to the Office of Sheriff, in favour of Mr. Rodham Kenner." [19]
These personal arrangements were, however, ineffectual unless approved by the county court, for the choice of local
officials lay with the justices. True enough, they were required
to name three men for the office of sheriff, one of whom the
governor would commission; but if the court had a preference

it did not hesitate to indicate its desires to the governor. For example, the court of Botetourt County, when recommending Captain Israel Christian and two others for the office of sheriff in 1770, enclosed a communication from Christian "asking for the Commission; ... and enclosing certificate, that only two of the Court voted against his recommendation."[20] In general, however, the court simply presented in order the three names highest on the commission of justices, passing over those who had already served as sheriff or who did not desire the office,[21] and the governor ordinarily commissioned the first of the three men named in the recommendation. In effect, therefore, this extremely important county official was the oldest justice in point of commission who had not previously held the shrievalty; and he could be expected to reflect the will of the court while performing his important duties, which included the management of burgess elections.

Near the middle of the eighteenth century there were between ten and fifteen justices in most of the counties.[22] Although the office of justice brought neither salary nor fees, its dignity and power made men eager to secure it, and the number of justices increased through the years. By the late 1780's the average number of justices in the county was 22; the range was from 11 to 36.[23] In the nineteenth century the commissions of the peace in the several counties were to become even more unwieldy in size.

For conducting routine business four of the justices were a quorum, and often no more than four were present. The personnel of the bench changed from day to day and from session to session, sometimes by prior agreement, so that no one justice was unduly burdened and so that all had a share in the business of the court, though naturally some were more active than others. For performing acts of extraordinary importance, such as ordering the erection of public buildings, determining the levy to be made upon the tithables of the county, or electing important officials, it was required that a majority of all the justices be present.

The court met monthly on a day fixed by law.[24] The first Monday in each month was a favorite time, though other Mondays and other days of the week were assigned to the various counties for court day. Sometimes the business was disposed of in a day; more often the court continued in session for several successive days but seldom for more than three.

On every third month the county justices convened as the Court of Quarter Sessions to deal with criminal cases in which the punishment of a free person did not extend to loss of life or limb. But the distinction between the quarter court and the county court was little more than a division of business under two different schedules. The same men presided over both courts, and the expression "county court" will therefore be used to include any and all of the monthly meetings of the county justices.

Court days were important occasions in the economy and society as well as in the government of the rural Virginia counties. The business of the court brought men to the county seat; others came because the assemblage of farmers and planters made this a convenient time and place for transacting private business. Sales of land and houses, hogs and cattle, were made on court day,[25] a practice which led the day to be called sales day in South Carolina. These monthly gatherings gave welcome relief from the isolation and loneliness of country life. No other institution in the eighteenth-century Virginia county was so colorful, lively, and variously important as court day, and the tempo of activity was much increased on those rare occasions when a hotly contested election was added to the usual business of the day.

Intelligent Virginians were well aware of the antiquity, the importance, and the extensive power of their county courts. Benjamin Watkins Leigh declared in 1819—and his remarks would have been equally valid a hundred and more years earlier—that the county court, "as it is the most ancient, so it has ever been one of the most important of our institutions, not only in respect to the administration of justice, but for police and economy." Since the seventeenth century, so he observed, the courts' functions have "been so important, that their institution may well be considered as a part of the constitution, both of the colonial and present government. No material change was introduced by the revolution in their jurisdiction, or general powers and duties of any kind. . . . It would perhaps be impossible for any man, to estimate the character and utility of this system, without actual experience of its operation." [26]

The laws reveal much about the operation of the county courts, but the records of the courts, especially the Order Books, give more insight into their activities. They show very clearly that the court, despite its name, was a legislative, executive, and electoral, as well as a judicial body. Separation of powers, and checks and balances, were unknown in Virginia county government. Every variety of governmental power was vested in the single body known as the county court.

The business disposed of by the Albemarle County Court in a twelve-month period, beginning with the September term, 1791, is a fair sample of the activities of these courts. It will be remembered that this was the county of Jefferson

and, at this time, of Monroe, though neither was during this
year an active member of the court.[27] Within this twelve-
month period the court was in session some twenty days. Its
activities, rearranged somewhat, included admitting to record
a large number of legal papers. Among these were an ac-
knowledgment of right of dower, indentures of bargain and
sale, deeds of mortgage, powers of attorney, last wills and
testaments, executors' bonds, and inventories of estates.

Once during the year a grand jury was sworn and charged,
and upon its return with several presentments, "Processes
were ordered to be issued." A large number of cases, both
civil and criminal, were tried, sometimes with a jury though
more frequently without one. Suits for debt were common;
damage and trespass cases were fairly frequent. In both of the
two more serious criminal cases the accused were slaves.
Davie was accused of stealing bacon, fifty pounds of beef, a
barrel of meat, clothes, and leather. Though charged with
felony, the court adjudged him guilty of a misdemeanor, and
ordered that he receive thirty-nine lashes on his bare back
and that "the Sheriff do execute this judgment accordingly."
In the second case, the slave Ben, charged with poisoning a
fellow slave, was found guilty of felony. Being allowed
benefit of clergy, he escaped the death penalty but was sen-
tenced to be burned in the hand.

Administering the general business of the county consumed
much of the court's time. Thomas Garth, one of the two
commissioners of taxes was allowed $57.57 for his services
and 7s 6d for paper. Orders were issued for paying witnesses,
with the amounts stated in terms of tobacco. Because English
and American monetary systems as well as tobacco were in
use, the justices had to think in terms of three kinds of cur-

rency. As part of their control over the collection of taxes, the justices approved lists of insolvents and exempted certain infirm slaves from taxation. James Garland, upon giving bond and security, qualified before the court as sheriff of the county, and two "sub-sheriffs" were also qualified. The court settled claims against the county submitted by the clerk, the sheriff, the jailor, and others, including a claim made by John Blackwell for 200 pounds of tobacco "for one old woolfs head."

Among its numerous activities aimed at maintaining roads and at keeping natural waterways navigable, the court appointed Philemon Snell "Surveyor of the Road from a Marked Tree on Eppersons mountain to where it falls into the Norfolk Road," with some fifteen designated "male laboring Tythes for his gang." It appointed a jury to view a mill site and a committee to inspect and report on the "Conveniences and Inconveniences" of a proposed new road. On another occasion the court requested each justice to list the overseers of roads with their boundaries and gangs in his part of the county.

The court received bonds and applications for licenses from those who would keep taverns and set in precise terms the amounts that tavern-keepers could charge for a gill of rum, brandy, or whiskey, for a gallon of oats or corn, for dinner or breakfast, and for "Lodging in a Feather bed per night." The court also appointed two persons "to inspect and try the scales and weights belonging to the warehouse at Milton," and from time to time it appointed inspectors of tobacco and received reports from them.

Several times within the year the Albemarle County Court exercised its right to elect other county officials. It evidently expected the resignation of John Nicholas, Sr., from the office of county clerk, for the unusually large number of twelve justices were present when it was submitted. At once they proceeded by unanimous vote to elect John Nicholas, Jr., formerly deputy clerk, to succeed his father. The two Nicholases held the clerkship of Albemarle County continuously for sixty-six years.[28] Long service in this office and the choice of a son to succeed his father were frequent occurrences in the clerkship of the Virginia counties.

At the next session of court a letter was received from Nicholas Lewis in which he declined "acting as a Justice of the Peace in this County," and two months later Thomas W. Lewis also withdrew from the bench. Upon receiving these resignations, the court did not immediately make its recommendations to the governor. However, several times within the year it nominated persons to be commissioned as militia officers, and it appointed persons to supervise elections of overseers of the poor.[29] The overseers were the only elective officers of the county, and this office had been in existence only since the disestablishment of the church in 1785. Somewhat later the court appointed overseers of the poor in two of the four districts of the county, presumably because elections had not been held.

Matters pertaining to the welfare of orphans and paupers occupied much time. The court appointed guardians of orphans and executors of estates, and it received and placed on record numerous guardians' reports. In one instance the ward was Meriwether Lewis, who later attained fame as Jefferson's secretary and as a leader of the Lewis and Clark expedition. On another occasion a guardian was given permission to bind his ward to Wilson C. Nicholas, Esq., until he should become twenty-one years old "to learn the art and mistery of a miller." That such arrangements needed to be closely supervised is indicated by a petition brought to the court on behalf of an orphan boy, Tom, bound to Richard Woods. After hearing this petition, the court ordered that Tom should not wear a collar, probably of iron, and that Woods should reimburse the petitioner for his costs.

In cases of illegitimate children the court sought to safeguard the welfare of the child and to protect the county from undue expense by placing the cost of supporting the child upon the father. In one instance it bound the father in the sum of £5 a year for six years for the maintenance of his bastard child, and it ordered him, upon his failing to furnish bond, into the custody of the sheriff. In another instance, an illegitimate girl was bound to Joseph Holt on motion of one of the overseers of the poor. Aged paupers as well as helpless youth looked to county government for assistance. At one of its sessions the court ordered that the names of several persons be placed on the list of pensioners, each to be allowed £12 a year.

In dealing with these matters of charity and morals in the years 1791 and 1792, the Albemarle County Court was performing duties recently acquired from the parish vestry. Prior to the disestablishment of the church in 1785, such duties, as well as the construction of churches, the maintenance of ecclesiastical property, the supervision of spiritual affairs, the employment of ministers, the processioning of land according to the ancient custom for maintaining property boundaries, and the fixing of tithes to support the work of the parish were the responsibility of vestries. The vestry sometimes spent more money than the county court. In the years immediately before the Revolution, Truro and Fairfax parishes, into which

Fairfax County was divided, each had larger budgets than the county budget.[30]

The business of each parish was conducted by twelve vestrymen who were required by law to meet twice a year. Throughout the eighteenth century the vestry was a self-perpetuating body, itself electing new vestrymen as vacancies occurred.[31] The vestries had also acquired the power of electing parish ministers despite complaints from the clergy, opposition by governors and commissaries, and the episcopal character of the church.[32] The Established Church, like civil government in Virginia, was thus broken into small units. In each of these spheres, ecclesiastical as well as political, government was conducted by a dozen or so men who had the power to choose their own successors.

The vestries with all their autonomous power were in no sense checks upon the county courts, for both bodies were dominated by the same men. George Washington, George Mason, and George William Fairfax, justices of Fairfax County, were vestrymen of Truro Parish.[33] Four of the nine vestrymen of Wicomico Parish who met on November 10, 1757, were justices;[34] and five of the nine vestrymen of South Farnham Parish who met on October 13, 1773, at Captain James Edmondson's at Piscataway Ferry, were justices.[35] Throughout the colony a large share of the justices and higher political officers were vestrymen. Bishop William Meade affirmed, "and that not without examination, that there was scarce an instance of any but a vestryman being in the Council," and that there were not three members of the Virginia Convention of May, 1776, who were not vestrymen of the Established Church.[36]

The disestablishment of the church in 1785 diminished the

power of one institution, the vestry, and enhanced the power of another, the county court; but it did not appreciably shift the location of power in society. Control over both institutions was lodged in the same segment of society and to a large extent in the very same men.

These men often possessed other forms of political power in local affairs. Mason and Washington, for example, were trustees of the town of Alexandria, and they and their fellow trustees conducted its affairs with approximately the same authority and power as were possessed by the magistrates of the counties.[37] The militia system was also under the firm control of the men who composed the magistracy. The fact that the county courts possessed the power to recommend to the governor all of the local militia officers creates a presumption that militia officers would be acceptable to the justices. As a matter of fact, the court frequently arranged for its own members to secure the higher offices. These were, in descending order, the county lieutenant, the colonel, the lieutenant colonel, and the major. In Albemarle County in the late 1780's, two of the ranking militia officers were justices and another was a kinsman of one of the justices. The situation in this county was general throughout the state. In some counties, as in Northumberland, all of the four ranking militia officers were members of the court.[38] Vestry, militia, and court were separate organizations; but the separation of ecclesiastical, military, and civil functions could not constitute a system of checks and balances so long as one man could hold office concurrently in all three organizations and often did.

The gentry of the county, operating through the county court, the vestry, and the militia, managed the business of the county and influenced the lives of their neighbors in many important respects. In local affairs, the members of the gentry were the government; and it was they who applied to local problems, both public and personal, such laws and policies as the provincial government had adopted.

CHAPTER SEVEN

The House of Burgesses

AMERICAN DEMOCRACY owes much to the diligence of the Virginia burgesses in defending their privileges and controlling the avenues through which men gained entrance to the House. But the burgesses were less concerned with the future of democracy through the long sweep of history than with immediate considerations of power and political advantage. It was self-interest that made them hold their ground in a long series of contests with the royal governor, and self-interest as well as a sense of political order led them to give close attention to burgess elections. After nearly every general election several seats were contested, and the decision between the contestants sometimes hinged on the acceptance or rejection of no more than two or three votes. The power to seat one contestant rather than another was useful to the leaders of the House in strengthening their position and in hindering the growth of a rival faction. But even if it was nothing more than a desire for power and for personal advancement that kept the burgesses at their task, the result of their labors was a precise and orderly body of rules for the conduct of elections; and this code, hammered out on the anvil of experience, was a contribution to democracy.

Democracy was also strengthened by the enlargement of

the powers of the elected branch of government at the expense of those of the royal governor. The power of the House increasingly overshadowed that of the governor during the colonial period, and in Virginia the American Revolution may be regarded as the natural climax of this trend. After the new state government had been formed, the executive branch was completely subordinated to the legislative. Jefferson asserted in the early years of statehood that the powers of the Assembly were despotic,[1] and St. George Tucker declared that "the executive department in Virginia, is *chosen, paid, directed,* and *removed* by the legislature. It possesses not a single feature of Independence." [2] The first state Constitution did not sharply separate the executive from the legislative branch of government though it provided "That the legislative and executive powers of the State should be separate and distinct from the judiciary." [3]

The subordination of the governor to the Assembly during the early years of statehood was accomplished in several ways. Comparatively few powers were granted to his office, his selection was vested in the legislature, his term was for a single year, and most of his powers could be exercised only with the advice and consent of the council of state. The legislature had ample means of restraining the council from straying far from the course that the legislature considered proper. Its eight members were chosen in the first instance by joint ballot of the two houses. At the end of each three-year period two councilors, presumably those least acceptable to the legislature, were removed from office by the Assembly. Their places as well as vacancies created by death or otherwise were filled by joint ballot of the two houses.[4] Those who held the office of governor showed little dissatisfaction with their subordinate position. Nearly all of them, as well as nearly all the members of the council, had served in the legislature. They normally represented the point of view of the majority of its members, otherwise they would not have been elected. It would not be far wrong to regard the governor and council as the executive of the Assembly rather than of the state.

The power of the Assembly in determining policy, in managing elections, and in filling a growing number of offices gave it a preeminent position in the politics of eighteenth-century Virginia. In the colonial period it was useful for a man with political ambitions to have the friendship of the governor; it was also useful, and indeed essential, for him to obtain a seat in the House of Burgesses. If he wanted great influence and high office, he had to understand the structure of the House and the processes by which men gained power within it.

The chief officers of the House were its speaker and clerk. Although the treasurer and attorney general were, strictly speaking, officers of the colony rather than of the House, those who filled these offices during the latter years of the colonial period were members of the House and wielded much influence in it. A remarkable feature of all four of these offices was the long tenure of those who held them. John Robinson became speaker and treasurer in the year 1738, just two years after he had entered the House; and he held both offices until his death in 1766—a tenure of twenty-eight years. Thereafter, these offices went to different men. Robert Carter Nicholas became treasurer for the remaining ten years of the colonial period. Peyton Randolph, who had held the office of attorney general for eighteen years, followed Robinson as speaker, and he continued in that office until his death in 1775. When Peyton Randolph left the attorney-generalship, his successor was his younger brother, John, who had served some years earlier as clerk of the house. Thus, from 1738 to 1775 the speakership was held by only two men, John Robinson and Peyton Randolph. During these same years only Robinson and Nicholas held the office of treasurer. From 1748 to 1776, there were only two attorney generals, first Peyton and then John Randolph. To this list of powerful men should be added the name of George Wythe, who became clerk of the House in 1769 after having served on most of its important committees.

Judged by their offices as well as by other indications of their power, Robinson until his death in 1766, Peyton Randolph, Nicholas, and Wythe were men of great influence in the House of Burgesses through the last fifteen years of the colonial period.[5] Other men may have been jealous of their power, but if so they were unable to break it. Indeed, there is little evidence that their power was ever seriously challenged except by Patrick Henry, and his victory on questions of policy caused no political heads to roll. These great men of the house held office as long as they wanted to hold it, and that was for a long time. So far as the scanty records show, they did not have to fight a series of parliamentary battles to stay in power. The processes by which office was secured and held are illustrated by events after the death of Speaker Robinson. Two men were nominated to succeed him, Peyton Randolph and Richard Bland. Each had served long and in prominent ways in the House, and their views on public questions were similar. Randolph was elected. When the House was organized after the next general election, Bland did not renew his struggle for the speakership. Instead, he himself nominated Randolph.

Randolph was reelected without opposition, and thereafter his tenure of the speakership was unchallenged.

The record of committee memberships also suggests that there was no opposition party or faction strong enough to take power from those who had once secured it. Most of the business of the House was managed by five standing committees; in 1769 the number of standing committees was increased to six. The most important of these in the eminence of the names on its roster and in the critical nature of its duties was the Committee of Privileges and Elections. Its membership was large, increasing from fifteen in the year 1761 to thirty-eight in the year 1772. Even larger and somewhat busier was the Committee of Propositions and Grievances which contained about half of the members in attendance in each session of the House and dealt with a host of local matters. Most of the private legislation had been prepared by this committee. The Committee on Religion, created in 1769, was about as large as the Committee of Propositions and Grievances. The other three standing committees were only about half as large as the first three. They dealt respectively with courts of justice, trade, and public claims. Most of the important business of the House was prepared and managed by these six committees, and if a man would have influence in the House he must have influence in these committees.

The chairmanship of the standing committees was seldom changed. Peyton Randolph presided over the Committees of Privileges and Elections and of Propositions and Grievances before he became speaker. Robert Carter Nicholas was chairman of the Committee on Religion during most of the years he was treasurer. These two men and five other burgesses monopolized the chairmanships of all of the six standing committees from 1761 to 1774.[6] Besides Randolph and Nicholas these men were Richard Bland of Prince George, Benjamin Harrison of Charles City, Edmund Pendleton of Caroline, Richard Henry Lee of Westmoreland, and Archibald Cary of Chesterfield. Except for Speaker Randolph, each of these men served on two, or more usually on three, standing committees in addition to the one of which he was chairman. And they dominated the numerous special committees created to deal with various matters. In the session of 1773, for example, the chairmen of the six standing committees were chairmen of twenty-one of the thirty special committees. Robinson, Randolph, Wythe, Nicholas, Bland, Harrison, Pendleton, Cary, and Richard Henry Lee, these nine men, reduced to eight after Robinson's death, controlled nearly every committee, special or standing. They were undoubtedly the leading men of the House.

There were nine others who were also powerful, though to a less degree, during all or nearly all of the years under consideration: Dudley Digges of York County, Lemuel Riddick of Nansemond, Thomas Whiting of Gloucester, Charles Carter of Lancaster, Lewis Burwell of James City, Francis Lightfoot Lee of Loudoun and Richmond, William Digges of Warwick, Patrick Henry of Louisa and Hanover, and George Washington of Fairfax. Each was a member of three of the standing committees, including in every case the committees of Privileges and Elections and of Propositions and Grievances. None, however, was chairman of one of the standing committees.

Although no hard and fast lines divided the burgesses into various levels of importance, it is clear that men were of unequal influence in the House. The reasons why some succeeded better than others are in large measure beyond analysis, though family connections, friendships, intellectual strength, and diligence all played a part. Length of service was certainly an element in advancement. As new members entered the House they were assigned at once to committees, and as the years passed their names moved upward in committee rolls. Except for adding the names of new members and dropping the names of those who had died or failed of reelection, the committee rosters changed but little. Rarely did a man who continued in the House leave a committee to which he had once been assigned unless, as occasionally happened, he had a heavy load of assignments and gave up one to accept a place on a more important committee.

But advancement to the first places on a committee and eventually to its chairmanship did not come by length of service alone. Sometimes a man newly arrived in the House was given more important assignments than members some years his senior. Thomas Mann Randolph and Thomas Jefferson were placed on the committees of Privileges and Elections and of Propositions and Grievances as soon as they became burgesses, showing that a man's career in the House was in some measure determined before he had participated in any of its deliberations. Some men rose to committee chairmanships with remarkable rapidity. Jefferson, for example, became chairman of the Committee of Propositions and Grievances after only six years in the House, and Joseph Jones reached the chairmanship of the Committee on Courts of Justice three years after he became a burgess, each going ahead of men with greater seniority.

Men differed in the heights to which they rose and in the rapidity of their progress, but they were alike in being subject to the benevolent rule that power, once it was attained, could be held without interruption. No committee chairman was reduced in rank between 1761 and 1774. In 1769 the membership of most of the standing committees was enlarged, which may have shifted the balance of power somewhat; and in 1775 the chairmanship of four of the important committees was changed. Harrison, Pendleton, Richard Henry Lee, and Bland were replaced by Dudley Digges, Thomas Jefferson, Joseph Jones, and Thomas Nelson, Jr.; but this drastic change in committee chairmanships did not reflect a revolution in the House. The burgesses had chosen the first four of these men, together with other of the ablest and most experienced burgesses, to represent Virginia in the Continental Congress and then had filled the posts they had formerly held in the House. The rule that power, once attained, could be held without interruption was not abrogated, but with the beginning of national political life an opening was made at the top through which some men passed from leadership in the House to positions in national affairs. As a consequence, advancement within the House became more rapid.

So long as the House was dominated by its older and more experienced members, as it was during the last fifteen years of the colonial period, prudence advised new members to work with rather than against the established leaders. The most notable case in which a new member of the House disregarded prudential considerations and challenged the leadership of those in power occurred in the year 1765, and Patrick Henry was the principal in the case. This episode as well as earlier events in his political career illuminates in an unusual way some of the tensions between an ambitious young man and the older men of experience and power.

Henry first attracted public attention in December, 1763, when he appeared before the Hanover County Court in opposition to an attempt of the clergy of the Established Church to secure payment of their salaries in tobacco at its market value instead of at a lower figure. By a brilliant appeal to the prejudices and emotions of a jury that included three or four dissenters and a large number of men who did not belong to the gentry, Henry won a verdict that was most displeasing to the clergy. One can only guess at the thoughts and feelings of Henry's uncle, who was a clergyman of the Established Church, and of his father, who was presiding justice of the court before which the case was argued.[7] But there is no doubt that he attracted much attention to himself by attacking the interests of the clergy, offending the instincts of conservatives, and opposing a strict interpretation of the law.[8]

One year later, in November, 1764, Henry stood before a smaller but a far more discerning group of men when he appeared before the Committee of Privileges and Elections of the House of Burgesses as counsel for Nathaniel West Dandridge. Dandridge was one of the leading justices of Hanover and he had served his county as burgess for some years,[9] but he had been defeated in the recent election by James Littlepage who was not a member of the county court.[10] Henry introduced evidence to show that Littlepage treated the voters to large quantities of food and drink, solicited their votes on a house-to-house canvass, criticized governmental policy in respect to tobacco inspection, made extravagant campaign promises, and, in general, infracted the code of proper political conduct as well as the provisions of the law. By opposing these practices of Littlepage and by appearing as the counsel of

Dandridge, Henry now appears as the champion of dignity and conservatism and of a scrupulous compliance with the law —a somewhat contrary position to that in which he had placed himself in the Parson's case.[11]

Henry's shift from a radical position to a more conservative one may have been due to nothing more than the attempts of a young lawyer to earn honest pennies from all who would pay for his services, regardless of their political views or social position. But it is also possible that he was trying to ally himself with the older and more influential gentlemen of his county with a view to beginning his own political career; there was a rumor during the Dandridge-Littlepage campaign that he was contemplating standing a poll.[12] If he was in fact planning a typical political career, beginning with the friendship of the local gentry, seeking election to the House with their aid and trying to rise to power in the House by winning the confidence and favor of the older burgesses, his share in the Dandridge-Littlepage contest placed him in a disadvantageous position. The faction in Hanover with which he was associated was defeated; and the elder statesmen of the House who controlled the Committee of Privileges and Elections, such men as Bland, Randolph, Wythe, Harrison, and Pendleton, were less favorably impressed by the young lawyer than the Hanover jury had been. The Committee's report, which was accepted by the House, was against Dandridge. To add salt to Henry's wound, the Committee described the case which he had presented as "frivolous and vexatious"! [13]

Just six months later Henry was in the House leading a successful, double-barreled assault on the position of the old leaders. He had been elected from Louisa County rather than from his home county of Hanover. It is sometimes said that he chose to run in Louisa because it was nearer the frontier, and that Henry was better qualified to deal with frontiersmen than with eastern planters. Perhaps so; but two things must be remembered. While Louisa was in fact just west of Hanover, it was not so far west as Jefferson's Albemarle, Madison's Orange, or Frederick that first sent Washington to the Assembly. Yet these three men were not typical frontiersmen. They were, rather, members of the gentry, and they rose to power with the support of the influential men of the locality. In the second place, Henry may have stood for office in Louisa for the simple reason that an election was held there earlier than in Hanover. William Johnson, one of the burgesses of Louisa, vacated his seat by accepting the office of coroner. A writ for a special election of a single burgess was issued; Henry became a candidate; and in less than three weeks he was presumably a member of the House, for on May 20, 1765, he was added to the Committee for Courts of Justice.[14]

Within ten days Henry had an influential part in blocking the creation of a loan office which would have concealed the misuse of public funds by John Robinson, Speaker of the House and Treasurer of the Colony. Some of the great men of the East who had profited from Robinson's indiscretion were much embarrassed that the loan office was not created.[15] At nearly the same time Henry introduced a set of radical resolutions against the Stamp Act, he supported them with his famous speech that brought forth cries of "Treason," and he carried most of them, though by a narrow margin.[16]

Henry's great powers as an orator helped him to win this victory, but his triumph was made easier by the absence of two thirds of the members from their seats during the closing days of the session. Even so, his victory during the first weeks of his membership was remarkable. According to Jefferson, he "took the lead out of the hands of those who had hitherto guided the proceedings of the House, that is to say, of Pendleton, Wythe, Bland, Randolph, Nicholas," and, he added in another account, of Speaker Robinson.[17] Except for Robinson, these were the men whose names were highest on the committee that six months earlier had branded Henry's presentation of the case of Nathaniel Dandridge as "frivolous and vexatious."

The old leaders were shocked and angered by their defeat: Peyton Randolph was heard to mutter as he left the House that he would have given a hundred guineas for another vote. But their rule was not ended; they had to give ground but they were not destroyed. Jefferson, who once referred to them as the "cyphers of the aristocracy" and in a kindlier mood as "honest and able men," explained that their reluctance to act rapidly and vigorously was due "to their age and experience." Their younger opponents, Henry, the Lees, the Pages, Mason, Jefferson himself, and others, "often wished to have gone faster," but, Jefferson continued, "we slackened our pace, that our less ardent colleagues might keep up with us; and they, on their part, differing nothing from us in principle, quickened their gait somewhat . . . and thus consolidated the phalanx which breasted the power of Britain."[18]

The division in the House at the time of the Stamp Act controversy was based on geography as well as on differences in age and experience. Henry's supporters were chiefly from the middle and upper country;[19] the old leaders were from the Tidewater, and most of them lived within fifty miles of Williamsburg.[20] But sectional antagonism was not an unsurmountable barrier to cooperation. Western counties sometimes reached back eastward for burgesses, as Hampshire County did when it elected Thomas Bryan Martin or Frederick County when it chose George Washington. The East, in turn, did not use its superior power over the West despotically. It carried a larger share of the tax burden, partly by placing a higher value on eastern land for purposes of taxation and partly by taxing slaves, who were more numerous in the East.[21] In the Piedmont, land and slaves were the material elements in success just as they were in the older East; and those who were building fortunes in sight of the Blue Ridge were of the same level of society and often of the very same families as those who dominated the Tidewater.[22] Throughout the eighteenth century most assemblymen, whether western or eastern, were planters, slaveholders, Episcopalians, and members of old families; and time was lessening the differences between Piedmont and Tidewater. In the nineteenth century a new society was to develop in the mountains of western Virginia that would never conform to the patterns of life in the East, but it was not large and strong enough to play a significant part in eighteenth-century politics.[23]

Although Henry's manners and habits may have best suited the society of frontiersmen and plain farmers, in the House he was dealing chiefly with gentlemen. Here was no case of a demagogue leading the poor people of the upcountry to victory over the periwigged gentry of the East. There were too many gentlemen in the House of Burgesses to be over-whelmed, and many of them lived west of the counties that Henry represented. By his victory he showed that he could exert influence inside the governing class of Virginia.

Sectionalism and differences of age caused tensions among

the burgesses, but these did not harden into permanent party alignments. Under pressure by younger and western members, the older, eastern leaders neither surrendered completely nor held their ground so obstinately as to cause their own political destruction. They made some changes in direction and in pace, but they kept a firm hold on the powerful offices of the House for many years before, during, and after the Revolution. Through these years the upward progress of a young burgess seldom began, as it did in the case of Henry, with a challenge to established authority. Instead, it usually began by working with those already in power and by gaining influence in the existing structure of politics rather than by attacking it from the outside.[24]

The continuance of this political system owed much to the willingness of the older men to recognize young talent when they saw it and to admit it into the partnership of power without long delay. The county justices sometimes supported the candidacies of young men. Madison and Jefferson were elected burgess when they were twenty-five, Monroe when he was twenty-four, and Washington when he was twenty-six. As soon as they reached the House some of these young men were immediately assigned to two or three of the most important committees, and those who showed promise were quickly loaded with responsibilities. Jefferson, almost immediately after entering the House, was complimented by being assigned the important task of drafting an address to Governor Botetourt. To his chagrin, Robert Carter Nicholas disliked what he had written and rewrote the paper himself,[25] but this difference of opinion between a young burgess and an elder statesman is less important than the general tendency that it illustrates. The old leaders, secure in their power to correct and overrule, readily tested the capacity of newcomers to the House. Those who made a favorable impression—as Jefferson did despite this episode—were soon advanced to higher responsibilities. The composition of the Committee of Correspondence and Inquiry, created on March 12, 1773, illustrates the rapid advancement of some of the younger members to partnership with the most powerful of the burgesses. In addition to Speaker Randolph and the chairmen of the six standing committees, the Committee consisted of Dudley Digges, Dabney Carr, Patrick Henry, and Thomas Jefferson.

As the years passed, it became increasingly difficult to see traces of the conflict that had existed between radicals and conservatives at the time of the Stamp Act controversy. If any division continued, neither group carried it to the point of excluding its opponents from high office. When the Virginia Convention of 1774, which was the House of Burgesses meeting without the governor's approval, elected delegates to the first Continental Congress, it chose Peyton Randolph, Richard Bland, and Edmund Pendleton from among those who had been known earlier as conservatives, and at the same time it choose Richard Henry Lee and Patrick Henry from among their former opponents. In the first years of the Revolution the Assembly elected Patrick Henry and Thomas Jefferson to the governorship while the lower house was choosing Edmund Pendleton, George Wythe, and Benjamin Harrison as its successive speakers. The members of the legislature seem to have forgotten that there had ever been a difference between radicals and conservatives.

Upon reaching the legislature, the Virginia politician was not at the pinnacle of success, but he had reached the only platform from which higher political careers could be built. He had become a member of a powerful electoral body, and his name had been placed, as it were, in the list of candidates for all of the many important offices at the disposal of that body. It was not a long list. There were not many more than a hundred seats in the House of Burgesses in the 1760's, and from the members of that House came nearly every Virginian who earned a name for himself in American history during the next quarter of a century.

The Assembly chose those who held high places in the state and most of those who represented Virginia in national affairs in the revolutionary and early national periods.[26] None were elected by direct vote of the people except members of the Assembly itself and, after the adoption of the Federal Constitution, of the lower house of Congress. The freeholders sent men to the Assembly, but only the Assembly sent men to higher places. Of state officials it elected the governor, members of the council of state, judges of the supreme court of appeals and general court, judges in chancery, and the secretary, the treasurer, the attorney general, and some others. It appointed all officers of the army and navy raised under the authority of the state, and militia officers above the rank of a field officer.[27] Most of the state's representatives in national affairs were also chosen by the Assembly. In the revolutionary period, delegates to the Continental Congress and to the Federal Constitutional Convention were thus chosen. After the establishment of the Federal government the legislature elected United States senators and, through the caucus system which soon developed, it spoke for Virginia in nominating presidential candidates. With this multiplication of offices after the colony became a state, the legislature sometimes depleted its own membership in the first days of the session by a tenth or more to fill the posts at its disposal.

In exercising its vast electoral power the Assembly seldom chose a man who had not served in the Assembly, and it usually chose from its present membership. All of the first ten governors of the State of Virginia, of the seven Virginia signers of the Declaration of Independence, and of the five Virginia delegates to the Federal Constitutional Convention had been members of the Assembly except Edmund Randolph. So it was with the representatives and senators from Virginia in the first and second Congresses, the early members of the council of state, and those who served as President of the United States or in the Cabinet during the early years of the nation. There were very few men who attained an important civil office without first serving an apprenticeship in the Assembly. The rare exceptions to the strict letter of the law by which men rose to high power complied with its spirit; through family connections, through Revolutionary War activities, and otherwise they began their careers by winning the approval and support of the men of weight and influence in the Assembly.

No one can prove, of course, that the Virginia legislature chose more wisely than the voters could have done in direct elections. But it is the verdict of history that the Assembly chose remarkably well, and the assemblymen certainly knew more about the strength and weakness of the leading men of Virginia than most of the voters could have known. By observing each other in deliberations and in committee work they had first-hand knowledge of George Mason's clear and profound thinking about the nature of government, of James Madison's knowledge of constitutional history, of Peyton

Randolph's trustworthiness and urbanity as a presiding officer, of Thomas Jefferson's skill with his pen, of Francis
Lightfoot Lee's excellence in committee though he was shy
and inarticulate in large groups, of Patrick Henry's superb
oratory on great occasions and of his inattentiveness to routine
business in the early stages of his legislative career. Knowing
these things, the burgesses made remarkably wise choices. To
the Continental Congress, for example, they sent Peyton
Randolph who was made its presiding officer, Henry to stir it
to action, Jefferson to draft the Declaration of Independence,
and Washington to be made head of the American military
forces. Unless one assumes that a host of Virginians were
equally well qualified to perform a number of critically important tasks, the conclusion is inescapable that the Virginia
burgesses were well informed and wise in selecting men with
such excellent and varied talents.

The burgesses knew what they were doing far better than
the voters in general could possibly have known with the
exception, perhaps, of the choice of Patrick Henry. His skill
in stirring men with the spoken word could be experienced
by men generally, and it was indeed well known. If the
Assembly's electoral powers had been vested directly in the
people, there is every reason to believe that Henry would
have profited by the change more than James Madison, Peyton Randolph, Francis Lightfoot Lee, Thomas Jefferson,
George Washington, and others who were as well, though
differently, qualified to serve the public.

CHAPTER EIGHT

The Pathway to Power

IN EIGHTEENTH-CENTURY Virginia there was only one pathway for a man to follow from the level flats of private life to the heights of political power, and seldom did anyone with political ambition stray far from it. Of the many who began the upward climb, few reached the peak; for on the road there were three narrow and closely guarded gates. To get through, a man had to show that he possessed certain qualifications, and the requirements changed from gate to gate.

In most cases the first upward step in a political career was admission to the office of justice of the peace and thus to a seat on the bench of the county court. Washington, Jefferson, Madison, Monroe, Wythe, and Mason as well as a large majority of Virginians who were signers of the Declaration of Independence, delegates to the Constitutional Convention, early congressmen, cabinet members, presidents of the United States, governors, or other high state officials entered this office near the beginning of their political careers. In the late colonial and early national periods more than three-fourths of the members of the Assembly had at some time been commissioned as justices of the peace.[1] John Marshall and Patrick Henry are among the few who reached high office without first serving in a county court, but they, and nearly all others who attained power without being commissioned as a justice of the peace, were members of families that were prominent in local politics.

Inasmuch as all local offices, ecclesiastical and military as well as civil, were secured through the influence of members of the gentry, it was nearly impossible to begin a political career without being in the gentry or closely connected with it. It was also most difficult for a radical or unpredictable gentleman to begin a career; for the gentlemen justices, who had the power to grant or refuse admission to the initial offices, generally had a conservative attitude toward society, economy, and government. Older laws sometimes referred to them as "conservators of the peace," and, in a broader sense than the law intended, this term was most appropriate. In recruiting for office, they chose from their own class in society young men of talent and promise who could be counted on to maintain the existing order.

Having passed the first testing point on the political pathway by securing the approval of the local gentry, the young justice began his practical education in the school of government as a member of the county court. Here the curriculum was broad, embracing civil and criminal cases, administrative problems, the fixing of local tax rates, and the election of county officials. The novice was not secluded in a private office with reference books about him; but, like an apprentice, he was seated with several of his older and more experienced colleagues while transacting the daily routine of public business. Thus, youth learned from age, and age formed an opinion of the diligence and ability of the new member of the court. On the basis of this opinion, the older members of the court could retard or accelerate the political advancement of the younger justices.

The work of the county court kept the justices in close touch with life. They saw the effect of general policies, set by the court and by Williamsburg, on the lives of individual men and women. Before them came the rich man seeking to evade listing his carriage for taxation, the tavern keeper charged with abusing an apprenticed orphan, the slave indicted with poisoning his fellow slave, the farmer complaining about poor roads. Nearly all of the Virginians who helped establish the rules under which the Commonwealth of Virginia should operate and who had a large share in setting the Federal system upon its course had seen the faces of men and women, children and old people, freeholders and slaves, when the power of government was applied to their individual lives. In eighteenth-century Virginia men learned to administer law and observed the effects of law before they were entrusted with its making.

From the county court the rising young politician usually went to the House of Burgesses. To become a burgess, he had to win the approval of the voters in a county election. Because it was expected that a candidate be educated, lavish in treating, and proper in his campaign methods, few outside the gentry could aspire to a seat in the House. Only rarely was a candidate not a gentleman. But all gentlemen were not equally likely to succeed in burgess elections. To win, they needed to have certain qualities and mastery over certain arts—qualities and arts that were not entirely like those useful in later periods of American history.

In burgess elections, oratory was of little or no advantage, and speech-making of any kind seems to have been rare during campaigns. When James Madison "addressed himself in a Speech to the people [of Orange County] in defense of the new Constitution" [2] in the year 1788, he was doing something unusual; and so was James Littlepage when he spoke to the voters of Hanover County long enough to retract extravagant promises he had made earlier in his campaign. After all, it would have been a bit ridiculous for a candidate to make high-flown, fulsome speeches to the several hundred men of his county who usually had known him for many years.

In the House of Burgesses oratory was more useful, for there politics was so constructed that votes could be turned this way or that by persuasive arguments. Ears were not deafened by party discipline nor were men compelled to vote as a party caucus had determined. And the burgesses were too well insulated from their constituents by distance and rudimentary means of communication to be immediately accountable for their day-by-day speeches and votes. Oratory was not necessary for reaching the highest places in the House; Bland, Peyton Randolph, and Robinson were all ungraceful speakers according to Jefferson,[3] and he might properly have added his own name as well as the names of Washington and Madison to this list of men who were statesmen without being orators. Nevertheless, skill in oratory was useful to the burgesses, for in the House they addressed men who were not closely controlled either by party or by constituents.[4] They could therefore speak as parliamentary orators, seeking to sway and convince their hearers; there was little temptation to use the trick of speaking across the shoulders of their hearers to their constituents back home. In the House of Burgesses a premium was put on oratory but not on demagoguery.

Oratory was more useful in the House than it was in campaigns to get to the House. While he was seeking office, the candidate had to stand up to the voters, individually and in small groups. He had to walk among the people at treats and on the morning of the election, greeting friends and acquaintances, answering questions, meeting criticisms, and on occasion holding his ground before a blustering, drunken opponent. During the polling he must face the voters with dignity and force. The oft-used phrase, that a man "carried his election," meant something more than mere success. There was an implication that success was deserved and earned by energy, force of character, ready information, manly presence, and courage.

Burgess elections gave office to those members of the gentry who could in this sense carry an election. Burgess elections also favored men who were on agreeable, friendly terms with persons in many walks of life. There was the temptation, to which some of the candidates yielded, to assume a pose of unusual affability as election day approached. Commenting with bitterness on this sort of behavior, a Pennsylvanian wrote in the year of American Independence: "A poor man has rarely the honor of speaking to a gentleman on any terms, and never with familiarity but for a few weeks before the election. How many poor men, common men, and mechanics, have been made happy within this fortnight by a shake of the hand, a pleasing smile, and a little familiar chat with gentlemen who have not for these seven years past condescended to look at them. Blessed state which brings all so nearly on a level! ... In a word, electioneering and aristocratical pride are incompatible." [5]

Plain men were not easily fooled by such behavior, especially in small and stable constituencies like the Virginia counties where the candidate's year-in-and-year-out manners and attitudes were too well known to be forgotten while he was campaigning. Men who were customarily haughty, aloof, and ultra-conservative might win the support of a few powerful gentlemen and thus gain seats in the county court; but in burgess elections the friendship and goodwill of the generality of men were needed. The House of Burgesses was made up of gentlemen, but only of gentlemen who were acceptable to ordinary men.

The will of the people was exerted upon government chiefly through the Assembly, and elections gave the voters their strongest instrument for making that body responsive to their wishes. There were other ways, of course, for the voters to tell their representatives what they wanted. Persons and organizations sent large numbers of petitions on many subjects to the Assembly; the disestablishment of the church, for example, was preceded by numerous petitions from Baptists and Presbyterians.[6] The ancient right of petition was a much-used democratic device in eighteenth-century Virginia. Nevertheless, in the last analysis it was popular elections rather than petitions or any other practice that gave the freeholders power to compel the Assembly to heed their wishes.

The double screening of the Virginia burgesses, first by the gentry and then by the freeholders, helps to account for an unusual and valuable quality in many of Virginia's political leaders. They had the talents, training, and experiences of the gentry; at the same time they had more zeal for representative government and for the general good of society than one might expect among representatives of a privileged class.

Having reached the House of Burgesses the Virginia politician dealt with larger and more general problems than those that had come to his attention in the county court. There were negotiations and then war with Indians and French, and there were problems of currency and taxation, of religion, transportation, staple crops, and land tenure. Controversies with the governor compelled the burgesses to think about the balance of power within a government; and quarrels with Great Britain raised fundamental questions about the relationship between the parts and the whole in a complex political structure. Later, the constitutional thoughts stirred up during the train of events leading to the Revolution were put to constructive use in establishing a republican system of government and the American Federal Union.

Although one or another of these important questions was sometimes the subject of a full-dress discussion, the House more often was busy with things which may have seemed of small import to some of the new burgesses, such things as the phrasing of an address to the governor and questions of ceremony in dealing with him, the decision to appoint or not appoint a committee, the sending of the sergeant-at-arms to compel burgesses to attend the sessions of the House, minute details of county elections, and the weighing of personal qualifications when appointing the committees of the House and selecting delegates to assemblies in Philadelphia and New York. To the newcomer, the House seemed to spend most of its time on small, routine matters; but the experienced legislators knew the importance of settling small matters with large goals in view. To win the approval of these leaders of the House, new members had to demonstrate an understanding of this fact.

If, after gaining experience and knowledge in committees

and on the floor of the House, a burgess demonstrated to his colleagues that he was thoughtful and diligent, ready in debate, skilled in oratory, learned in parliamentary procedure, gifted in drafting state papers, or able to see the distant tendency of immediate problems, he might be chosen speaker of the House, a delegate to the Continental Congress or the Federal Constitutional Convention, governor of Virginia, a member of the Council, or a United States senator.

Neither the 35,000 or 40,000 voters nor the 300 or 400 families that dominated the county courts had sole power to send men to the House. Each had a share in this essential operation, and each had to make some adjustments to the opinions and desires of the other. A man came to the Assembly only if he had strong support in both of these groups, and his characteristics reflected this fact. Once in the Assembly his subsequent career was almost entirely determined by his fellow assemblymen, those who were better informed than the voters could ever be about his qualities and his behavior in office. The nature of Virginia's political leadership and of the leadership that Virginia supplied to the nation was profoundly influenced by these forces that selected men and advanced them to the highest offices. It was also influenced by what these men had learned about the art of politics at each stage of their upward path as they progressed from county court to Assembly and then from Assembly to higher offices.

CHAPTER NINE

The Eighteenth Century
to the Twentieth

JUDGED BY THE quality of the men it brought to power the eighteenth-century-Virginia way of selecting political leadership was extremely good; but judged by modern standards of political excellence, it was defective at nearly every point. As for voting qualifications, there was discrimination against women, poor men, and Negroes. There was no secrecy in voting, and polling places—only one in each county—were spaced too far apart. The two-party system was not in existence. Local government was totally undemocratic, and few offices at any level of government were filled by direct vote of the people: only burgesses in the colonial period and not many other officers for many years after the Revolution. Such modern refinements of political processes as the nominating primary, initiative, referendum, popular recall, proportional voting, and mechanical voting machines were, of course, unknown.

Nearly every detail of the political processes of eighteenth-century Virginia has been repudiated; but, at the same time, the men elevated by those processes have come to be regarded as very great men. Here is a dilemma in an area of fundamental importance, and its resolution is no simple matter. Was eighteenth-century Virginia so full of great men that a random selection would have provided government with a goodly supply of great statesmen? If not, must it not follow that the selective system played an important part in bringing to the top the particular men who managed the public affairs of that day?

Any appraisal of the system that elevated the revolutionary generation of Virginia leaders to power must take account of the society and economy in which it operated. At that time Virginia was comparatively free from competing groups. True, there were tensions between planters and Scottish merchants, between adherents of the Crown and revolutionists, and between officials of the Established Church and dissenters; but in the main, eighteenth-century Virginia was remarkably homogeneous. The overwhelming majority of men were agriculturalists, differing in the scale of their operations more than in the nature of them. They were trying to get ahead on parallel rather than on conflicting lines. Nearly every burgess was a representative of agriculture; there was little else in Virginia that he could represent. Under these circumstances, those who achieved most in non-political life could be vested with political power without seriously endangering the interests of less successful men. It was more or less appropriate for the large planter to represent the small farmer, and the farmer accepted this leadership as natural and proper.

All this is not to say that gentlemen of eighteenth-century Virginia were less vain, less ambitious, or less selfish than men have generally been. They demonstrated an active interest in their own advancement when they decided to stand an election for the House of Burgesses, selected the county in which to offer themselves, treated the voters, cultivated influential men, and placed themselves before the freeholders during the hours of decision.[1] But the circumstances of the times diminished the opportunity for ambitious, selfish men to prey upon society through the use of political power. In this agrarian society government hardly touched man's chief means of livelihood, agriculture. Those who gained control over the law-making processes therefore had little opportunity to enrich themselves at the expense of others.

This much is plain: the political system of eighteenth-century Virginia was admirably suited to the social order which existed in eighteenth-century Virginia. And the political devices used, no matter what their theoretical value for other times and places, made this political system work. The system brought such men as Washington and Jefferson into politics and allowed them to reach the top. One device which is considered objectionable today, the colonial practice of letting a man sit in the Assembly for a county where he was not a resident, gave to Henry, Washington, and others their first opportunity to enter the House of Burgesses. Virginia profited by an early beginning of the careers of these men; and sectional tensions in Virginia were perhaps diminished by this practice which lasted until the Constitution of 1776. Though Washington lived in Fairfax County, he must have felt some obligations to the freeholders across the Blue Ridge in Frederick County who had sent him to the House. And there were others like him whose outlook in public matters was probably broadened because they were attached to the interests of more than one locality.

Another device, the practice of requiring voters to be property owners, is even more bitterly condemned by present day political standards; but the critics of the property-holding requirements for voting too often lose sight of the ideas and purposes behind the requirements and forget what they accomplished. They are usually interpreted as an attempt to disfranchise the poor and deliver government into the hands of men of property. But the words of the law itself,[2] the modest amount of land required for voting, and the comments of contemporaries indicate that the prime object of the law was to restrict the political power of the very rich. As one Virginian expressed it, "the object of those who framed the constitution of Virginia was to prevent the undue & overwhelming influence of great landholders in elections," by disfranchising their landless "tenants & retainers" who depended "on the breath & varying will" of these great men.[3] And there was another object of more fundamental importance. It was, in the words of the Constitution of 1776, to enfranchise those men, and only those, who had a "permanent common interest with, and attachment to, the community." The ownership of land was obviously not a perfect index in the eighteenth century, and it would be far less perfect now. But it must be remembered that the electorate which gave its assent to the political advancement of these Virginia leaders and which was at the foundation of government in revolutionary Virginia was drawn only from the men of property.

One might even argue that a combination of bad practices on election day in colonial Virginia—oral voting, treating, and long journeys to the courthouse—came nearer to producing a working democracy than have the more rational and sophisticated devices of a later day. The prospect of refreshments and of an exciting day in which the humblest voter could play his public part brought out a high per cent of the electorate. The voter was given a simple task, and it was performed in a fashion that heightened his awareness of his political importance. In the colonial period his only duty was to elect burgesses, and sometimes he was called upon to elect them only once in three years. All of his political attention was focused upon choosing two men out of a list of three, four, or perhaps five candidates.

If he chose well, the voter lost little by trusting his representatives to select other officials. And if the voter's judgment was sound, there was no reason why he should not make a good choice because he usually knew each of the candidates personally. In the colonial period the county was the largest constituency in Virginia, and very few counties contained as many as a thousand voters. In the years when the great generation of Virginians were beginning their political careers, the voter, whether he were wise or foolish, whether his motives were lofty or ignoble, usually knew what he was doing when he decided for one man and against another.

The voters, as voters generally are, were subjected to pressure in these elections. In colonial Virginia, as always, men of wealth and power exerted extraordinary influence in politics. But in the political system of eighteenth-century Virginia there was a frank and open recognition of this condition and a large measure of public knowledge as to how it was operating in particular cases. When Lord Fairfax supported Washington, his support was open and clearly recognizable; voters were not kept in the dark about the connection between the several candidates and the powerful men of the community. True, the voters were subjected to pressure and they were subjected to some forms of pressure that have since been minimized; but the pressure was comparatively open and unconcealed.

Pressure on the voters at election time came mostly from

the county courts. These courts were neither efficient, learned, nor democratic. All too frequently they gave judicial decisions with little knowledge of the law, and they were beyond effective control by the people of the county. But paradoxically, these undemocratic courts served democracy well because they could resist pressures brought to bear on them from Williamsburg and later from Richmond. They served as a firm anchor of power down at the bottom of the political structure. Ancient custom, re-enforced after statehood by constitutional provisions, placed county government in some measure beyond colonial or state control.

The semi-independent status of the counties had long-run effects on American history as well as immediate effects on the choice of political leadership in Virginia. Those Virginians who helped draft the Federal Constitution had lived under a quasi-federal system in colonial Virginia. They were thoroughly familiar with the little citadels of power located in each of the counties. They had seen the advantages of strongly fortified local positions during conflicts with the king's representatives at Williamsburg. The experiences of these men in Virginia politics and government must not be forgotten when reflecting on the origins of the American federal system of government.

In assessing the importance of the political power of the county courts a comparison of the history of Virginia and South Carolina in the first half of the nineteenth century is valuable. Of the two, South Carolina, with its secret ballot, its more generous suffrage provisions, and its avoidance of self-perpetuating, gentry-controlled county courts was the more democratic; yet South Carolina became the more ardent defender of slavery, the advocate of nullification and secession, and, in the eyes of many, a great threat to the American democratic experiment.

The reasons for this apparent paradox are complex; but among them is the fact that South Carolina's government, though more democratic than Virginia's, was much more centralized. The foremost champion of states rights had made scarcely any provision for county rights—certainly none equal to those in Virginia. There were no autonomous local offices in South Carolina where Union men could entrench themselves and live out the storm of the nullification controversy. The party that gained control over state government was able to deprive its opponents of nearly every office and instrument of power.[4] In Virginia, in contrast, men and parties could win or lose power in Richmond without the county courts being much shaken by these changes. The magistrates could continue to exert much influence over the choice of representatives in the legislature. So long as the courts continued, Virginia never experienced a drastic political revolution; power was never seized by inexperienced men; and the people were never brought under the control of a centralized power. The courts were undemocratic, but they served democracy well.

Such vestiges of aristocracy in eighteenth-century Virginia as property qualifications for voting, oral voting, the power of the gentry in elections, and the arrogation of virtually all offices, local and state-wide, by the gentry, are contrary to twentieth-century principles and ideals of democracy. It is nevertheless certain that the high quality of Virginia's political leadership in the years when the United States was being established was due in large measure to these very things which are now detested. Washington and Jefferson, Madison and Monroe, Mason, Marshall, and Edmund Randolph were products of the system which sought out and raised to high office men of superior family and social status, of good education, of personal force, of experience in management; they were placed in power by a semi-aristocratic political system.

All this is not to say that the electoral processes of colonial Virginia would be good for another time and place. But these considerations suggest that the path of political change needs occasional re-examination to see whether innovations have worked as well as their advocates prophesied and to search for useful elements in outmoded systems—values that may have been unwittingly destroyed and forgotten.

As a matter of fact, the undemocratic features of eighteenth-century Virginia politics did not go uncriticized in their own day. Thomas Jefferson, who was a member of the gentry and whose rise to power was through the channels controlled by the gentry, was nevertheless an outspoken critic of the arrangements to which he owed so much. His criticism stemmed in part from his belief that the gentry was sometimes an obstacle to progress. He blamed the justices for obstructing his plan to establish publicly supported elementary schools, explaining that "the members of the [county] court are the wealthy members of the counties; and as the expenses of the schools are to be defrayed by a contribution proportioned to the aggregate of other taxes which every one pays, they consider it as a plan to educate the poor at the expense of the rich." [5]

This experience reinforced Jefferson's long-standing dislike for the monopoly of power over local government by a small, self-perpetuating body of men who came nearly always from a small number of leading families.[6] Since the preeminence of these families was based on their large holdings of land, Jefferson devised a plan to whittle down their political power by diminishing their economic power. He drafted legislation that abolished entails and primogeniture, and he took much pride in thus laying "the ax to the foot of pseudo-aristocracy." [7]

Two things must be remarked about Jefferson's attack upon the political leadership of the Virginia gentry. In the first place he was seeking a gradual rather than a sudden change. Of more importance, in fact of supreme importance, he showed no disposition to leave a vacuum in political leadership. The principle of relying on heredity to produce leaders —and this is what he meant by the term "pseudo-aristocracy" —he distrusted not because this principle was then working badly but because he believed it must in the long run work badly. He therefore sought to destroy this method of finding leaders; but with equal earnestness he strove to persuade his fellow Virginians to adopt another plan that would discover and prepare for public responsibilities what he called the "natural aristocracy."

To discover and train political leaders Jefferson put his faith in an educational system of his own devising. Not much of his plan was adopted in his day, and since his day the plan has never been tried in America; for the Jeffersonian plan was more than a hierarchy of state-supported schools devoted to educating youth. An integral part of it was a series of screenings that would permit only the most exceptional youth to proceed from grade to grade until he reached the highest level of state-supported education. It began with small, local schools where boys would be given three years of elementary education in reading, writing, and arithmetic. Each year "the boy of the best genius, in the school, of those whose parents are too poor to give them further education," was to be sent up to one of the twenty grammar schools to be established in the state. Here there was to be a second rigorous selection. After trial of a year or two, the ablest boy was to be chosen out of all who came to each school in a given year. He was to be "continued six years, and the residue dismissed. By this means," so Jefferson observed, "twenty of the best geniuses will be raked from the rubbish annually, and be instructed, at the public expense, so far as the grammar schools go." Even this was not the end. There was to be a third screening after the six years of grammar school, and only those who passed this final test were to be educated at state expense at the university.[8]

From the standpoint of the twentieth century, Jefferson's plan seems severely if not harshly rigorous. Nearly all who entered the lowest grades would be dropped by the wayside before the highest level of education was reached. But it must be remembered that Jefferson was destroying no educational opportunity then in existence. In his day parents paid for the education of their children, and he would let them continue to do so as much as they wished. Instead of subtracting from this arrangement, he would add to it the opportunity for every child, no matter how poor, to receive an elementary education; and if the child proved to be superlatively able, he would receive without cost the most complete formal education that Jefferson could devise. To the eighteenth century, Jefferson's plan seemed to be a long and generous step forward; it was too much of a step for his Virginia contemporaries to take.

Jefferson was doubtless pleased by the thought that children of poor parents would be greatly helped by his plan. But in his public utterances he emphasized public benefits rather than assistance to needy persons. The state, he reasoned, should support education because education would benefit democracy. His plan would give at least the elements of education to all voters, and in its upper brackets it would train "able counsellors to administer the affairs of our country in all its departments, legislative, executive and judiciary, and to bear their proper share in the councils of our national government." [9] By this system "worth and genius" would be "sought out from every condition of life, and completely prepared by education for defeating the competition of wealth and birth for public trusts." [10]

The destructive half of Jefferson's great plan for revising the quality of political leadership was adopted; steps were taken to end leadership by the aristocracy of birth and wealth. But the constructive half of his plan, which sought to fill office from the natural aristocracy of talents and training, was not adopted. No one knows whether his whole plan would have worked, for it has never been tried. However, the plan itself seems to have had one glaring defect in it. His program might have discovered and trained talented men for public life, but Jefferson did not come to grips with the problem of how to get these men into office. The system he helped to destroy, despite all of its theoretical defects, actually put superior men in office. At this point in his own program, Jefferson is silent.

More important than any of the details of Jefferson's plan is the fundamental assumption behind it. The author of the great assertion "that all men are created equal" had no faith in the equal fitness of all men for political leadership. His educational plan was based on the assumption that men are unequal in natural talents and in the use to which they put such talents as they have. His political philosophy had as a cornerstone the idea that a democracy should be led by the best trained of its ablest men. Democracy, according to Jefferson, must have this kind of an aristocracy to lead it.

Although Jefferson's contemporaries did not support his plans for discovering and training superior men for office, they agreed that society needed the leadership of its ablest men and that it was the duty of men of this kind to seek and to hold office. Robert Munford made one of the characters in *The Candidates* declaim: "But, sir, it surely is the duty of every man who has abilities to serve his country, to take up the burden, and bear it with patience." [11] On the stage of real life this sentiment was echoed to Jefferson himself. Under a heavy load of domestic anxiety and distress, he wrote to Speaker John Tyler that he could not take the seat to which he had been elected in the Assembly. Tyler responded: "I suppose your [reasons] are weighty, yet I would suggest that good and able men had better govern than be governed, since tis possible, indeed highly probable, that if the able and good withdraw themselves from society, the venal and ignorant will succeed." [12]

Nearly two centuries have passed since these men entered public life. In this time democracy has made great gains in America, chiefly in the period that bears the name of Andrew Jackson. The number of voters has multiplied, elective offices have increased, the two-party system has evolved, and nominating and electoral techniques have been perfected. The goal of democracy has been lengthened and broadened to include new groups of oppressed or unfortunate people and to give help and assistance in ever-widening areas of life. The importance attached to this great and complex movement by American historians is demonstrated by the host of articles and books with such titles as the Growth of Democracy, the

March of Democracy, the Age of Democracy, the Frontier and Democracy, and the Evolution of Democracy.

Those who have written under these titles have said very little about mistakes and losses along the road of the democratic movement, perhaps because attention to these things might seem to imply disloyalty to democracy itself. But surely no one could object if Washington and Jefferson, Madison and Marshall spoke plainly about losses as well as gains in American self-government since their age. It would be presumptuous, of course, to attempt to speak for them; but surely it is not presumptuous to point out elements in their political system that seem to have been lost sight of or at least minimized with the passage of the years.

Their system of self-government was based on the idea that democracy and aristocracy are not mutually exclusive, and that both of these can and ought to be used by a self-governing people. In eighteenth-century Virginia the generality of men enjoyed certain political privileges and had certain political duties to perform, but the higher and more difficult political duties were placed upon men who stood above the general level. It was perhaps inevitable that as the privileges and duties of the common man were increased in later years, especially in the Jacksonian period, there should be a declining faith in the usefulness of aristocracy in politics and a greater self-confidence on the part of the average citizen in his own ability to hold office. And it has perhaps been natural for historians to write more about the growth of democracy than about the decline of aristocracy in American history.[13] But there is no reason to think that the great generation of Virginians regarded all men as political equals. They did not believe that a man who was qualified to vote was therefore fit to hold office. Jefferson's words and the political practices of his generation of Virginians plainly say that there is a place for a certain kind of aristocracy as well as a place for democracy in self-government.

Finally, the political system of colonial Virginia warns against too much preoccupation with the mechanics of democracy. The gentlemen-politicians of the eighteenth century showed little interest in reforming the machinery of self-government though the machine they used was by modern standards seriously defective. Since their day each generation has tried to improve and refine political processes. The caucus system of making nominations was evolved. In time it was replaced by the convention, and the convention by the primary. The secret ballot, universal manhood suffrage, woman suffrage, the direct election of United States senators and other officials previously appointed or indirectly elected—these and other changes have been made in the faith that each would bring democracy closer to perfection. Undoubtedly, many of these changes have been improvements; but perfection has not been reached. Perhaps Americans in their intense preoccupation with improving the form of self-government have forgotten more important matters.

It is worth recalling that this generation of Virginians did not delay doing essential tasks until they could reshape and perfect the political instruments at hand. They were not ignorant of some of the defects and crudities of their political processes; but they never lost sight of large public issues while they tinkered with the machine. They were wise enough to know that it could never be perfected to such a point that it would automatically turn out a good product. Rather, they regarded it as nothing more than an instrument that men could use, or fail to use, to accomplish good purposes. To them democracy was not like a snug house, purchased in full with a heavy payment of sacrifice at the moment of its establishment, and then to be enjoyed in effortless comfort ever after. Their concept of self-government included the idea that it was a burden, valuable but heavy, which must be borne constantly. Carrying this burden was to them more important than refining the forms of political processes; for they knew that if they or their successors ever laid down the burden, or in weariness permitted it to be taken from their shoulders by more willing but less worthy men, self-government would come to an end. They knew no way for democracy to work except for men of good will to labor incessantly at the job of making it work.

APPENDICES

APPENDIX I

Number of Voters in
Virginia Elections, 1741-1843

THE FOLLOWING table contains all county election statistics that have been found for the years 1741 to 1790 except in Essex and Westmoreland counties. In these, sampling was used. After 1790 statistics were added only for those counties listed in the earlier period. No claim is made for completeness or absolute accuracy, but perhaps the material is sufficient to show something about the number of persons who voted in county elections. In the colonial period these elections were all for burgesses; thereafter they were for state representatives and senators, delegates to state constitutional conventions, representatives to Congress, and presidential electors. If two seats were to be filled, as was the case in most burgess elections, the number of votes was twice the numbers of voters. The figures in this table show the number of voters.

The general trend in the number of voters participating in elections was downward. In 34 elections held in 14 counties from 1741 through 1772 the average number of voters was 313. Then in 1785 the church was disestablished, religion could no longer be a ground for disfranchisement, and an increase in the number of voters might be anticipated. Instead, there was a slight decrease; in 19 elections held in nine counties from 1786 through 1800 the average number of voters was 299. (The Essex County election in which only 19 persons voted for a presidential elector in 1792 was omitted from this group.) In 23 elections from

NUMBER OF VOTERS IN VIRGINIA ELECTIONS, 1741-1843

Year	Essex	West-more-land	Frederick	Spot-sylvania	North-umber-land	Fairfax	Other Counties
1741	325	322 [a]					414 [a] Prince William
1744							
1748		363		193 [d]		239 [b]	197 [a] Lancaster
1752		322				292 [c]	
1754		165					
1755		338					
1757			291 [b]				
1758			397 [c]		328	349 [c]	270 [a] Prince George
							121 [a] Elizabeth City
1761	368 [a]	306 [a]	601 [c]				
1765	368 [a]				342	256 [c]	578 Amelia
1768					157	207 [b]	399 [d] Fauquier
1769					362		
1771					289		
1772					337		331 [d] Lunenburg
							240 [b] Surry
							183 Stafford
1786					296		259 [e] Orange
							282 [a] Princess Anne
							282 Buckingham
1787	400						240 [e] Orange
1788					291		270 [a] Princess Anne

Year					
1789					209° Orange, 383° Orange, 231ª Princess Anne, 272ª Princess Anne, 359° Culpeper, 279° Albemarle
1792	19				
1793	393				
1794	234	280			661ᵍ Mecklenburg
1799		260			
1800		208			
1801		260			
1802		255			
1807		251			
1815		99	678ᵗ		
1823	240		737ᵗ		
1824	241, 247, 245	173, 193, 60		246	
1825	131, 245, 245	197, 191, 196			
1828		131, 197			
1829		95, 113			
1830		90			
1837		334, 339			
1843		288, 379			

1823 through 1843 held in three counties the average number of voters was 209.

The returns from Essex and Westmoreland counties, extending from the 1740's until well into the nineteenth century, are especially significant in showing this downward trend in the number of voters participating in elections. Population was not changing much; between 1790 and 1840 the white population of each county increased about ten per cent. The boundaries of these two counties were not changed in any important respect during the hundred years covered by these elections. Morgan P. Robinson, *Virginia Counties: Those Resulting from Virginia Legislation*, in Virginia State Library, *Bulletin*, 9 (Richmond, 1916), p. 168, and maps.

Most of the election returns were taken from photostatic or film copies of county poll sheets in the Virginia State Library. Others, indicated by letters, are from a variety of sources, namely:

a. Lyon G. Tyler, "Virginians Voting in the Colonial Period," in *William and Mary Quarterly*, 1st ser., 6 (1898), 7-14.

b. J. Franklin Jameson, "Virginian Voting in the Colonial Period (1744-1774)," in *The Nation*, 56 (April 27, 1893), 309-10.

c. MS. poll sheets in the George Washington Papers, Library of Congress.

d. *Journals of the House of Burgesses of Virginia.*

e. MS. Francis Taylor Diary in Virginia State Library.

f. Henry St. George Tucker to St. George Tucker, April 7, 1807, and April 4, 1815, in Tucker-Coleman Papers, Colonial Williamsburg, Inc.

g. A manuscript copy of the poll of a Mecklenburg election of April 14, 1794, in Duke University Library.

Population and Voting Statistics of Seven Virginia Counties, 1783-1790

THE DATE of the following table, which compares population and election statistics, was fixed by the year of the first Federal census. The choice of sample counties was determined by the availability of elections returns. These could be found for seven counties during the 1780's, and all of these fell in the years from 1786 to 1789.

The figures were taken from the following sources:

Columns 1 and 2. *Compendium of the Ninth Census* ... 1870 (Washington, 1872).

Columns 3 and 4. *Census of 1790.*

Column 5. The figures in this column were arrived at by counting the number of landowners listed in the manuscript land tax lists of the several counties, omitting women, orphans, and estates. The number of adult male owners of 25 or more acres should be approximately the number of qualified voters. The land tax lists are in the Virginia State Library.

Column 6. These figures are taken from Appendix I, the numbers for Orange and Princess Anne being in each case the average of four elections.

Column 7. The tax upon tithables was in effect a head tax. Under the law in force in 1786 (Hening, XI, 417-19; XII, 413) the tithable was a "free male person above the age of twenty-one who shall be a citizen of this commonwealth." Had the law been perfectly enforced, as it evidently was not, a list of tithables would give the number of white males of voting age, information which the census of 1790 does not give. The tithables are listed in the county personal property tax lists;

POPULATION AND VOTING STATISTICS OF SEVEN VIRGINIA COUNTIES, 1783-1790

County	1 Total Population 1790	2 White Population 1790	3 Free White Males under 16 1790	4 Free White Males 16 & over 1790	5 Male Landowners 1788		6 Voters in an election 1786-89	7 "Free Male Tithes" 21 & over 1783-85	8 Heads of Families
					Less than 25 acres	25 acres or more			
Albemarle	12,585	6,835	1,790	1,703	3	785	279	1,001	710
Buckingham	9,779	5,496	1,537	1,274	2	611	282	676	
Culpeper	22,105	13,809	3,755	3,372	8	935	359	1,786	
Essex	9,122	3,543	869	908	2	444	400	547	483
Orange	9,921	5,436	1,426	1,317	4	553	273	721	653
Princess Anne	7,793	4,527	1,151	1,169	32	579	264	870	827
Stafford	9,588	5,465	1,355	1,341	5	335	183	735	448
Total	80,893	45,111	11,883	11,084	56	4,242	2,040	6,336	

the county totals are brought together in Miscellaneous Records from the Auditor's Office, Accession 164 [49]. This document gives 58,169 as the number of tithables for the entire state which is less than two thirds of the number of adult white males as estimated in Chapter III, p. 31. There are strong reasons for thinking that many adult white males escaped taxation, especially those who were unattached, say as sons or hired laborers, to a landowner. The manuscripts mentioned in this paragraph are in the Virginia State Library.

Column 8. *Heads of Families at the First Census of the United States … 1790 … Virginia* (Washington, 1908). These were counted, estates and orphans being omitted.

A comparison of the totals of columns 2 and 6 indicates that between 4 and 5 per cent of the white population was voting in elections in the 1780's. Other students have put the percentage of voters in the last half of the eighteenth century slightly higher. After studying 13 county elections between 1744 and 1774, J. Franklin Jameson concluded that "about six per cent. of the white inhabitants of colonial Virginia voted." Jameson, "Virginian Voting in the Colonial Period (1744-1774)," in *The Nation*, 56 (April 27, 1893), 309-10. Lyon G. Tyler, using other colonial elections, found a higher percentage of voters, but two errors have been found in Tyler's calculations. Tyler, "Virginians Voting in the Colonial Period," in *William and Mary Quarterly*, 1st ser., 6 (1898), 7-13. Julian A. C. Chandler, comparing data in the *Richmond Enquirer*, November 21, 1800, with the census of 1800, concluded that in the presidential election of 1800 about 5¼ per cent of the white population voted. Chandler, *History of Suffrage in Virginia*, 21.

BIBLIOGRAPHICAL NOTE

Bibliographical Note

Four groups of material are described here because they support large segments of the discussion rather than being pertinent to single sentences or paragraphs.

LAWS

William W. Hening, *The Statutes at Large: Being a Collection of All the Laws of Virginia* . . . (13 vols., Richmond, Philadelphia, 1819-23), contains the election laws in force during the eighteenth century. The most important of these were passed in 1699, 1705, and 1736 (Hening, III, 172-75, 236-46; IV, 475-78).

Toward the end of the colonial period the Virginia Assembly enacted two more laws to regulate elections, one in 1762 (Hening, VII, 517-30) and the other in 1769 (*ibid.*, VIII, 305-17); but by their own terms neither of these was to become operative until approved in England. Approval by the Commissioners for Trade and Plantations seems to have been withheld: *Journals of the Commissioners for Trade and Plantations from January 1759 to December 1763 Preserved in the Public Record Office* (London, 1935), pp. 365, 369; *ibid.*, 1768-1775 (London, 1937), pp. 257, 345-46. Nevertheless, these two laws of the 1760's, even though they were not confirmed, are useful documents. They repeat with few changes the provisions of the earlier laws, thus indicating that the Assembly, which exercised supervisory power over election processes, continued to approve most of the rules that had been enacted near the beginning of the century.

After independence and before the end of the eighteenth century the following election laws were passed: An act of 1785 (Hening, XII, 120-27) concerning the election of delegates and senators to the general assembly; and acts of 1788 concerning the election of presidential electors (*ibid.*, 638-53) and representatives to Congress (*ibid.*, 653-57).

COUNTY COURT

Because the county court was founded on time-honored custom as well as on law, the description of local government in J. B. Black, *The Reign of Elizabeth, 1558-1603* (Oxford, 1936), pp. 174-77, comes fairly close to fitting Virginia local government in the late colonial and early national periods. An account of county government in early Virginia is in Philip A. Bruce, *Institutional History of Virginia in the Seventeenth Century* (2 vols., New York and London, 1910), I, 484-646, and in eighteenth-century Virginia, in Douglas S. Freeman, *George Washington* (New York, 1948—), I, 175-80, and Albert O. Porter, *County Government in Virginia, A Legislative History, 1607-1904* (New York, 1947), ch. II.

[Benjamin W. Leigh, comp.,] *The Revised Code of the Laws of Virginia* (2 vols., Richmond, 1819), I, 244-61, contains a revision into a single act of most of the laws governing the county courts. Other laws of less importance are elsewhere in this code, for example, I, 263, and II, 62-66. Brief and thoughtful comments on these matters are in St. George Tucker, *Blackstone's Commentaries: with Notes of Reference, to the Constitution and Laws, of the Federal Government of the United States; and of the Commonwealth of Virginia* ... (Philadelphia, 1803), bk. I, pt. 1, Appendix, pp. 115-16; and Thomas Jefferson, *Notes on the State of Virginia* (Richmond, 1853), 140-41, which was drafted in 1781 and 1782. A folded table, compiled for the years 1790-1791, gives much information about the Virginia counties and county courts. Further insight into the powers and activities of the county court comes from reading the records it created, especially the Order Books. Many of these and of other court papers are accessible in the Virginia State Library.

LISTS OF COUNTY, COLONIAL, AND STATE OFFICIALS

Lists of Virginia officials have been of much assistance in this study. Names of justices of the peace of the counties appear at several places in *Executive Journals of the Council of Colonial Virginia* (5 vols., Richmond, 1925—). The text and index of *Justices of the Peace of Colonial Virginia, 1757-1775*, in Virginia State Library, *Bulletin*, 14

(Richmond, 1922), were very useful. For the period between 1775 and 1860 there are in the Virginia State Library eight manuscript lists of justices and of some other county officials. Titles vary. The first volume is entitled "Commission Book No. 1"; the lists within it seem to have been made up in 1787 with additions and corrections to 1797. Later volumes are usually entitled "Register of Justices," followed by dates.

William G. Stanard and Mary N. Stanard, comps., *The Colonial Virginia Register* ... (Albany, N. Y., 1902), and Earl G. Swem and John W. Williams, comps., *A Register of the General Assembly of Virginia, 1776-1918* (Richmond, 1918), published with the Virginia State Library, *Fourteenth Annual Report of the Library Board* ..., *1916-1917* (Richmond, 1917), provide convenient lists of burgesses, state representatives and senators, and some other officials.

PLAYS

One of the best documents on elections in eighteenth-century Virginia was a play written about the year 1770 by Colonel Robert Munford of Mecklenburg County, Virginia. It was entitled *The Candidates; or, the Humours of a Virginia Election*, and it was first published at Petersburg, Virginia, in 1798. One hundred and fifty years later it was published again, with an Introduction by Jay B. Hubbell and Douglass Adair, in the *William and Mary Quarterly*, 3d ser., 5 (1948), pp. 217-57. *The Candidates* was given further circulation in the form of an offprint of the *William and Mary Quarterly* edition, and page references throughout this study have been to the offprint.

If this play were the only surviving record of its times one would hardly know how much faith to put in it. But inasmuch as most of its important points are corroborated in contested election cases in the *Journals of the House of Burgesses* and in other documents, *The Candidates* must be regarded as a remarkably reliable and interesting record. Munford knew what he was writing about. He had been a candidate for burgess more than once, and he was a member of the Assembly at the time that this play was probably written. If some allowance be made for the satirical character of the comedy and for Munford's earnest championship of righteousness, *The Candidates* can be accepted as an accurate reflection of the political spirit of the times as well as a description of the way eighteenth-century Virginians behaved at elections.

An English play with a political title but with less attention to politics than to affairs of the heart could be seen in Virginia in the 1790's. It was Sir Henry Bate Dudley's *The Rival Candidates: A Comic Opera in Two Acts; as It is Now Performing at the Theatre Royal in Drury-Lane. By the Rev. Henry Bate* (London, 1775). A copy is in the Henry E. Huntington Library. There is no resemblance between this play and Robert Munford's *The Candidates*, and Munford's play is a far more important document in the history of politics.

Dudley's *The Rival Candidates* was produced at the Southwark Theatre in Philadelphia on June 13, 1791. George O. Seilhamer, *History of the American Theatre: During the Revolution and After* (Philadelphia, 1889), 320-21. In December, 1791, it was played in Richmond, Virginia, and in 1795 in Norfolk. Susanne Sherman, Post-Revolutionary Theatre in Virginia (M.A. Thesis, College of William and Mary), 96, 270. See also Dougald MacMillan, *Catalogue of the Larpent Plays in the Huntington Library* (San Marino, 1939), no. 384.

REFERENCES

References

CHAPTER I
Behind the Virginia Dynasty

1. In this chapter the author is heavily indebted to the biographers of the leading men mentioned herein, and especially to Charles M. Wiltse, *The Jeffersonian Tradition in American Democracy* (Chapel Hill, 1935), 18-59, and to Dumas Malone, "The Great Generation," in *Virginia Quarterly Review*, 23 (1947), 108-22.

2. Paul L. Ford, ed., *The Writings of Thomas Jefferson* (New York, 1892-99), IX, 340 n, 466-70; and a checking, in the *Dictionary of American Biography* and other reference works, of the education of early Virginia officeholders.

3. John P. Kennedy, *Swallow Barn* . . . (New York, 1866), 35.

4. Some evidence on this point is summarized in Charles S. Sydnor, "The Southerner and the Laws," in *Journal of Southern History*, 6 (1940), 9-10.

5. Thomas Jefferson, *Notes on the State of Virginia* (Richmond, 1853), 173.

6. Jefferson to Edward Coles, August 25, 1814, in Ford, ed., *Writings of Thomas Jefferson*, IX, 477-79.

CHAPTER II
Tumults and Riots

1. H. R. McIlwaine, ed., *Journals of the House of Burgesses of Virginia, 1752-1758* (Richmond, 1909), 335. Hereafter cited as *J. H. B.*

2. *Ibid.*, xxiv-xxv.

3. *Ibid.*, 336.

4. *Ibid.*, 336-37.

5. *Ibid.*, 396-97.

6. *Ibid.*, 397.

7. Laws regulating elections can be consulted in William W. Hening,

The Statutes at Large; Being a Collection of All the Laws of Virginia...
(Richmond, Philadelphia, 1819-23), hereafter cited as Hening. For a
discussion of these laws see Bibliographical Note: Laws.

8. Writs for urban elections were directed to the sheriff of the appropriate
county. For example, writs for Jamestown and the College of William
and Mary elections were directed to the sheriff of James City County.
Hening, VII, 524-26.

9. The colonial election laws describe this procedure. Its operation in
Spotsylvania County in 1748 is set forth in detail in *J. H. B., 1742-1749,* pp.
292-93. A complete set of papers for a York County election in 1776 is in
a box labelled "Election Returns & Qualifications of Delegates to the
General Assembly at Williamsburg in the years 1776 & 1777" in Virginia
State Library.

10. *J. H. B., 1752-1758,* pp. 341-42.

11. *Ibid.,* 347.

12. *Ibid.,* 347-48, 381.

13. *Ibid.,* 446-47.

14. *Ibid.,* 447. The petition of Robert Porterfield, contesting the election
of William McCoy to the 14th Congress (House of Representatives files,
National Archives), describes a disorderly election in Rockingham County
in 1815.

15. For the length and breadth of Virginia counties in 1790, see folded
sheet at end of Jefferson, *Notes on Virginia.* For instances of stopping over-
night on the way to elections, see *J. H. B., 1761-1765,* pp. 271-72.

16. *Ibid., 1742-1749,* p. 292.

17. Jefferson to Joseph C. Cabell, February 2, 1816, Thomas Jefferson
Papers, Library of Congress.

18. Elkanah Watson, *Men and Times of the Revolution* . . . (2nd edn.,
New York, 1856), 71-72. Another account, written by a crank, of a
Virginia election is in Massachusetts Historical Society, *Proceedings,* 46
(1913), 370-71.

19. John C. Fitzpatrick, ed., *The Diaries of George Washington, 1748-
1799* (Boston and New York, 1925), I, 301. Hereafter cited as Washington,
Diaries.

20. Northumberland County, Record Book, 1756-1758, photostatic copy
in Virginia State Library.

21. For a sample of this procedure see the poll of the election in Buckingham County on April 14, 1788. A photostatic copy of these sheets is in
Virginia State Library, Accession No. 20059.

22. *J. H. B.*, *1742-1749*, p. 202.

23. Washington, *Diaries*, I, 344.

24. Diary of Francis Taylor of Orange County, vol. XIII, entry for April 24, 1799. Virginia State Library, Accession No. 18710.

25. The poll sheet, with "Objected" or "Obj" written after many names, is in Westmoreland County Records, Inventories, No. 2, 1746-1752, photostatic copy in Virginia State Library. The absence of any reference to this election in the *Journals of the House of Burgesses* is the basis for the supposition that Quarles decided not to take his dispute to the House.

Grounds for objections are illustrated in the contested election case of John Taliaferro v. John P. Hungerford for a seat in the 12th Congress (1811) as representative of the Northern Neck district of Virginia. These papers are in the files of the House of Representatives, in the National Archives.

26. *J. H. B.*, *1770-1772*, pp. 163, 251-52.

27. John S. Wise, *The End of an Era* (Boston and New York, 1899), 55-56.

28. This description is taken from George W. Munford, *The Two Parsons; Cupid's Sports; the Dream; and the Jewels of Virginia* (Richmond, 1884), 210.

29. *J. H. B.*, *1761-1765*, pp. 86-90.

30. George W. Munford, *The Two Parsons*, 210; *J.H.B.*, *1752-1758*, pp. 446-47; Robert Munford, *The Candidates; or, the Humours of a Virginia Election*, ed. with an Introduction by Jay B. Hubbell and Douglass Adair (Williamsburg, 1948), 32-33. See Bibliographical Note: Plays.

31. *J. H. B.*, *1758-1761*, pp. 84, 100.

32. Douglas S. Freeman, *George Washington: A Biography: Young Washington* (New York, 1948), II, 146. An alphabetical poll sheet of this election in Washington's hand is in the Washington Papers, Library of Congress. Among other close elections were the Elizabeth City contest discussed above, an election in Lunenburg County in 1771 in which the poll, after correction by the House of Burgesses, stood 166 to 165 (*J. H. B.*, *1770-1772*, pp. 251-52), and an election in Northumberland County on July 25, 1771, in which the final vote was 147 to 149 (Northumberland County Record Book, 1770-1772, pp. 271-73, photostatic copy in Virginia State Library).

33. Nicholas Cresswell, *The Journal of Nicholas Cresswell, 1774-1777* (London, 1925), 28.

34. These words are from Robert Munford, *The Candidates*, 43. This

procedure was prescribed in the colonial laws. For an illustration of its use, see *J. H. B., 1742-1749*, p. 293.

35. *Richmond Enquirer*, February 14, 1822.

36. Diary of Francis Taylor of Orange County, vol. IX, entries for April 27 and 28, 1795. Westmoreland County, Deeds & Wills, No. 26 [1828-1831], microfilm in Virginia State Library, pp. 114-18, records the vote for presidential electors continuing from November 3 through November 4, 1828. Hening, XII, 123, gives one of the laws on this subject.

37. Robert Munford, *The Candidates*, 43; *J. H. B., 1761-1765*, p. 89.

38. Washington, *Diaries*, I, 301; II, 43, 169; IV, 3.

CHAPTER III
The Vulgar Herd

1. Free Negroes amounted to less than two per cent of the aggregate population. Most of them would have been excluded by the landholding qualification. These statements are based on a wide sampling of the original county tax lists of the 1780's in the Virginia State Library, and on St. George Tucker, *Blackstone's Commentaries: with Notes of Reference, to the Constitution and Laws, of the Federal Government of the United States; and of the Commonwealth of Virginia* ... (Philadelphia, 1803), bk. I, pt. 1, Appendix, p. 100. In this edition the four "books" are published in five volumes. Hereafter cited Tucker, *Blackstone*.

2. Hening, IV, 477.

3. *J. H. B., 1761-1765*, p. 269.

4. *Memoirs of the Life and Peregrinations of the Florentine Philip Mazzei, 1730-1816*, translated by Howard R. Marraro (New York, 1942), 213-14. For a reference to Quakers as voters see Stanislaus M. Hamilton, ed., *Letters to Washington and Accompanying Papers* (Boston and New York, 1898-1902), II, 344.

5. Robert B. Woodworth, *A History of the Presbytery of Winchester, Synod of Virginia, ... 1719-1945* (Staunton, Va., 1947), 13.

6. *William and Mary Quarterly*, 2d ser., 8 (1928), 194. The poll sheets of this and some other Frederick County elections are in the Washington Papers, Library of Congress.

7. *Notes on Virginia* (1853 edn.), 169.

8. Appendix I.

9. The colonial assembly had written this change into law in 1762

(Hening, VII, 518), but the act had not been confirmed in England. See Bibliographical Note: Laws.

10. This complicated matter is summarized in Julian A. C. Chandler, *The History of Suffrage in Virginia* (Baltimore, 1901), 18-20.

11. *Heads of Families at the First Census of the United States Taken in the Year 1790, Records of the State Enumerations: 1782 to 1785, Virginia* (Washington, 1908), 10. Hereafter cited *Heads of Families, 1790, Virginia*.

12. *J. H. B., 1752-1758*, p. 359.

13. *Ibid., 1761-1765*, p. 88.

14. Hening, XII, 120-21. See Bibliographical Note: Laws.

15. This generalization is based on an examination of many land tax lists of the Virginia counties of the 1780's.

16. The only evidence I have seen that tenants were voting is in the "Diary of Colonel Landon Carter," in *William and Mary Quarterly*, 1st ser., 16 (1907-08), 260. Carter's statement is dated April 1, 1776.

17. Inasmuch as approximately 41 per cent of Connecticut white males were 21 and over in the year 1774 (calculated from *A Century of Population Growth from the First Census of the United States to the Twelfth, 1790-1900*, Washington, 1909, pp. 168-69) and 43 per cent of Virginia white males were in this age bracket in 1840 (calculated from *Sixth Census or Enumeration of the Inhabitants of the United States... in 1840*, Washington, 1841, p. 210), it may be assumed that not far from 42 per cent of Virginia white males, which would amount to 95,370, were of voting age in 1790. See also Appendix II, comments on Column 7.

18. Jefferson, *Notes on Virginia*, 127; Jefferson to John H. Pleasants, April 19, 1824, in Ford, ed., *Writings of Thomas Jefferson*, X, 303. The freehold requirement was changed in no important respect from the colonial period to the date of this letter; but the administration of the law and the percentage of landholders may have changed.

19. Governor Dinwiddie to the Lords of Trade, February 23, 1756, in R. A. Brock, ed., *The Official Records of Robert Dinwiddie* (Richmond, 1883-84), II, 345; Tucker, *Blackstone*, bk. I, pt. 1, Appendix, pp. 99-100.

20. Several estimates of the number of disfranchised are given in Chandler, *History of Suffrage in Virginia*, 26 ff. One man asserted that nine-tenths of the freemen were deprived of suffrage.

21. Appendix II is the basis for generalizations in this and the next few paragraphs.

22. The ratio in the 7 sample counties between 4,242 owners of 25 acres or more and 22,967 white males was as 1 to 5.4142. Applying this ratio to

the 227,071 white males enumerated in the entire state in the first Federal census shows 41,940 voters.

23. Hening, II, 82; III, 238.

24. Amherst County, Order Book, 1787-1790, p. 290. Amherst Court House. For this item I am indebted to Professor Robert D. Meade.

25. *Calendar of Virginia State Papers* (Richmond, 1875-93), VI, 419. For a petition of Chaney Gatewood, who had been fined in King and Queen County in August, 1796, for failure to vote, see *ibid.*, VIII, 382. See also, *J. H. B., 1727-1740*, p. 426.

26. *J. H. B., 1761-1765*, p. 271.

27. Tucker, *Blackstone*, bk. I, pt. 1, Appendix, p. 100.

28. Appendix I.

29. The charter is reprinted in Edgar W. Knight, *A Documentary History of Education in the South before 1860*, I (Chapel Hill, 1949), 397-439. See page 437 for the provision respecting a burgess for the College.

30. *Virginia Magazine of History*, 16 (1908-09), 109-10.

31. Essex County, Deeds, No. 41, 1823-[1828], microfilm copy in Virginia State Library.

32. *J. H. B., 1766-1769*, pp. 290-91. An instance of nonresident voting in Spotsylvania County is reported in *ibid., 1742-1749*, p. 293, but the number is not given.

33. Tucker, *Blackstone*, bk. I, pt. 1, Appendix, p. 100.

34. See Appendix II.

35. Based on a comparison of the land and personal property tax lists of Charles City County for 1787 in Virginia State Library.

36. For illustrations, see John Clopton to John Bacon Clopton, April 9, 1810, in Clopton Papers, Duke University Library, and *J. H. B., 1727-1740*, p. 426. The tax lists show scattered cases of sons with 50 acres.

37. Based on comparisons of the land and personal property tax lists of Northumberland County for 1786 and of Charles City County for 1787, all in Virginia State Library.

38. Section 6 of the Declaration of Rights, Virginia Constitution of 1776. Ben. P. Poore, comp., *The Federal and State Constitutions, Colonial Charters, and Other Organic Laws of the United States* (2d edn., Washington, 1878), II, 1909.

39. Based on a close examination of land tax lists of Essex, Princess Anne, and Stafford counties and a cursory examination of the lists of Albemarle, Buckingham, Culpeper, and Orange counties, all for the year 1788 or within a year thereof.

40. The estimate that perhaps a third of the voters owned no slaves is made partly on the basis of a scanning of the county tax lists and partly on the basis of a tenuous statistical calculation. It has been estimated that there were 34,026 slaveholding families in Virginia in 1790 (*A Century of Population Growth*, 138), but many of the owners were women, orphans, or estates; therefore the number of slaveholding men was considerably less than 34,026. The number of voters was larger, being probably between 35,000 and 40,000.

The statement that many slave owners possessed no more than one family of Negroes needs no further support than to say that the average number of slaves owned by a slaveholding family was 8.5. *Ibid.*, 138.

41. The number of qualified voters was not far below the number of heads of families: for every seven voters there were about eight heads of families. See Appendix II.

42. Jameson, "Virginian Voting in the Colonial Period (1744-1774)," in *The Nation*, 56 (April 27, 1893), 310.

CHAPTER IV
Swilling the Planters with Bumbo

1. See Bibliographical Note: Plays.
2. *The Candidates*, 17.
3. *Ibid.*, 20, 34.
4. *Ibid.*, 18.
5. *Ibid.*, 34.
6. Quoted in William P. Cresson, *James Monroe* (Chapel Hill, 1946), 92.
7. The quotations and a discussion of this matter are in Freeman, *Washington*, II, 318. Washington's vigorous campaigning three years later is described in *ibid.*, III, 61-62.
8. Henry St. George Tucker to St. George Tucker, April 2, 1807, Tucker-Coleman Papers, Colonial Williamsburg, Inc.
9. Same to same, April 7, 1807.
10. Same to same, April 4, 1815.
11. *The Candidates*, 27-28.
12. *J. H. B., 1761-1765*, pp. 269-71.
13. Douglass Adair, ed., "James Madison's Autobiography," in *William and Mary Quarterly*, 3d ser., 2 (1945), 199.
14. Madison to Washington, December 2, 1788, in Madison Papers, Library of Congress. See also Madison to Jefferson, December 8, 1788, and

other letters of this period in the Madison Papers. In the 1790's Madison became a more aggressive candidate.

15. "Diary of Colonel Landon Carter," in *William and Mary Quarterly*, 1st ser., 16 (1908), 259.

16. Entry of April 1, 1776. Robert Wormeley Carter kept his diary in an interleaved almanac now in Archives Department, Colonial Williamsburg, Inc.

17. Henry St. George Tucker to St. George Tucker, March 1, March 27, April 2, April 7, 1807, in Tucker-Coleman Papers.

18. Same to same, April 4, 1815. By this date Tucker's standards of political conduct were becoming old-fashioned.

19. *The Defence of Injur'd Merit Unmasked; or, the Scurrilous Piece of Philander Dissected and Exposed to Public View. By a Friend to Merit, wherever found* (n. p., 1771), 10. The Yale University Library copy of this rare pamphlet was used.

20. *J. H. B., 1761-1765*, p. 270.

21. *The Candidates*, 20-21, 29.

22. *Ibid.*, 29.

23. *Ibid.*, 23.

24. *Ibid.*, 43.

25. *Ibid.*, 30.

26. *J. H. B., 1761-1765*, p. 269.

27. *Ibid., 1752-1758*, pp. 360-61.

28. *J. H. B., 1761-1765*, p. 270. For another case of the investigation of campaign promises, see *ibid., 1752-1758*, pp. 360-61.

29. *The Candidates*, 22.

30. Letters of March 14, April 14, and April 19, 1812, in Clopton Papers, Duke University Library.

31. *Virginia Gazette* (Purdie and Dixon), November 10, 1763. This notice was called to my attention by Dr. Lester J. Cappon.

32. John Stokes Adams, ed., *An Autobiographical Sketch of John Marshall* (Ann Arbor, 1937), 15-16.

33. Charles Campbell, ed., *The Bland Papers* ... (Petersburg, 1840-43), I, 27. "Bumbo" was a slang term for rum.

34. Dumas Malone, *Jefferson the Virginian: Jefferson and His Time*, I (Boston, 1948), 130. For data on Washington and Marshall see below.

35. Munford in *The Candidates* tells of such a treat given on a race-field a day or two before an election. *The Candidates*, 19, 24, 26-27, 39.

36. Washington, *Diaries*, I, 301; II, 43, 169. Candidates, especially those

who had joined interests, sometimes tried to reduce expenses by giving a joint treat. Malone, *Jefferson*, I, 129-30.

37. *The Candidates*, 38-41.

38. *J. H. B.*, *1761-1765*, pp. 271-72.

39. Hamilton, ed., *Letters to Washington*, II, 397-400.

40. *J. H. B.*, *1752-1758*, p. 360.

41. *Ibid.*, *1761-1765*, p. 271.

42. Freeman, *Washington*, II, 320-21, using data in Hamilton, ed., *Letters to Washington*, II, 398-400.

43. George W. Munford, *The Two Parsons*, 208.

44. *J. H. B.*, *1727-1740*, p. 370.

45. *Ibid.*, pp. 426-27. For other attempts to secure votes by treating and pre-election promises see *ibid.*, *1758-1761*, pp. 82-84.

46. Hening, III, 243.

47. *Virginia Gazette* (Purdie & Dixon), July 7, 1774. This item was called to my attention by Dr. Carl Bridenbaugh.

48. "James Madison's Autobiography," 199; William C. Rives, *History of the Life and Times of James Madison* (Boston, 1873), I, 180-81.

49. Thomas Jefferson to James Madison, March 5, 1795, in Madison Papers, Library of Congress.

50. Letter, dated April 25, 1807, in Tucker-Coleman Papers.

51. *J. H. B.*, *1761-1765*, p. 272. For examples of the purchase of votes with liquor see *ibid.*, *1727-1740*, pp. 370, 426.

52. *Ibid.*, *1752-1758*, p. 360; *The Candidates*, 40-41.

53. *J. H. B.*, *1761-1765*, p. 272. See also *ibid.*, *1727-1740*, p. 370, and *ibid.*, 1758-1761, p. 83.

54. *Ibid.*, *1752-1758*, p. 360.

55. *Ibid.*, *1761-1765*, p. 272.

56. Washington to Colonel James Wood, [July, 1758], in John C. Fitzpatrick, ed., *The Writings of George Washington* ... (Washington, [1931-44]), II, 251.

57. Cresswell, *Journal*, 28. Washington was "the returned member." Charles Broadwater, the other successful candidate, had not previously served in the House.

58. *The Candidates*, 39.

59. "James Madison's Autobiography," 200.

CHAPTER V

Gentlemen of Long-Tailed Families

1. Ann Maury, *Memoir of a Huguenot Family* (New York, 1853), 419.
2. William Wirt, *Sketches of the Life and Character of Patrick Henry* (Philadelphia, 1818), 33-34. This appraisal of Virginia society was written by Thomas Jefferson though Wirt may have edited it. See Ford, ed., *Writings of Thomas Jefferson*, IX, 472-74.
3. George Tucker, *The Life of Thomas Jefferson* ... (London, 1837), I, 10-11; J. P. Brissot de Warville, *New Travels in the United States of America, Performed in 1788* (Dublin, 1792), 434, summarizing opinions of George Washington. Thomas Jefferson found himself surrounded with many examples of indolence and profligacy during his student days at Williamsburg. Malone, *Jefferson*, I, 52, 56, 87.
4. Hunter D. Farish, ed., *Journal & Letters of Philip Vickers Fithian, 1773-1774; A Plantation Tutor of the Old Dominion* (Williamsburg, 1943), 211-12.
5. *Memoirs of Philip Mazzei, 1730-1816*, p. 213.
6. *The Candidates*, 20, 26.
7. Jefferson to David Jameson, April 16, 1781, in Julian P. Boyd, Lyman H. Butterfield, and Mina R. Bryan, eds., *The Papers of Thomas Jefferson* (Princeton, 1950—), V, 468.
8. Dinwiddie to Colonel John Spotswood, November 2, 1757, in *Official Records of Robert Dinwiddie*, II, 711-12. The contractions in the Governor's letter have been expanded into full words.
9. Dinwiddie to James Abercromby, March 20, 1756, *ibid.*, II, 377.
10. Leonard W. Labaree, *Conservatism in Early American History* (New York, 1948), 6-10, 34-36; Carl Bridenbaugh, *Seat of Empire: The Political Role of Eighteenth-Century Williamsburg* (Williamsburg, 1950), 40-41.
11. From the opinion of Justice Blandford in *Bendheim Bros. & Co.* v. *Baldwin*, 73 Georgia 594 (September term, 1884).
12. In the lists of justices during this period, twelve family names occur ten or more times, namely, Anderson, Ball, Cocke, Harrison, Jones, Lewis, Payne, Robinson, Smith, Taylor, Walker, and Washington. Among the forty-three surnames that appear at least five times but less than ten times are Barbour, Campbell, Carter, Lee, Mason, Meriwether, Morton, Pendleton, Randolph, Taliaferro, Thornton, and Watkins. These statements are based on the lists and index in *Justices of the Peace of Colonial Virginia, 1757-1775*, in Virginia State Library, *Bulletin*, 14 (Richmond, 1922).

13. In the year 1788 there were 151 justices of the peace in these eight counties. Their total population was 78,159 of whom 47,139 were white and 31,020 black. Estimating the average family at six persons, one out of every 52 of the heads of white families was a justice of the peace. The sources from which these statements were derived are the United States *Census of 1790; Heads of Families, 1790, Virginia,* 3; "Commission Book No. 1" for the names of the justices; and county tax lists, both personal and land, for the year 1788 if they could be found for this year, otherwise for 1787 or 1789. The "Commission Book" and the tax lists, all in manuscript, are in the Virginia State Library.

The averages given above are probably too small because (1) justices are known to have omitted property from their tax declarations, for example, see Helen Hill [Miller], *George Mason: Constitutionalist* (Cambridge, 1938), 49-50; and because (2) these averages take no account of property outside the county of the justice's residence, whereas some of them had land and slaves in several counties. Although a few of the justices were comparatively poor, most of them were in the upper ten per cent of the economic scale of their counties.

14. For example, in Charles City County in the year 1788 there were thirteen persons, Mary Byrd and twelve men, each of whom was listed as owning 20 or more slaves above the age of twelve. Four of these were justices, and one of them, William Lightfoot, with 87 Negroes of taxable age, was the largest slaveholder in the county. In Northumberland County, five justices and the county clerk were among the fifteen persons owning 20 or more slaves above twelve years old. In Essex County the corresponding figures were 11 justices out of 31; in Halifax, 5 out of 9; in Albemarle, 4 out of 21; in Orange, 5 out of 14.

15. Freeman, *Washington,* II, 147, 317-21.

16. *Executive Journals of the Council of Colonial Virginia,* V (Richmond, 1945), 301.

17. Bishop William Meade, *Old Churches, Ministers and Families of Virginia* (Philadelphia, 1900), II, 285.

18. Two poll sheets for this election are in the Washington Papers, Library of Congress. One shows the voting in the order in which votes were given. The other, in Washington's hand, reveals his painstaking and practical interest in politics: he took the trouble to rearrange the ten-page, four-columns-to-the-page, poll into an alphabetical listing of those who voted for each candidate. Freeman, *Washington,* II, 320, gives a slightly different tabulation.

19. So it was before the American Revolution. The Constitution of 1776 required that a delegate to the Assembly be a resident of the county he represented, but the former custom of occasionally electing non-residents was not immediately ended. See the case of Benjamin Harrison presented below. Late in the year 1788 some of James Madison's advisors debated whether he should seek election to Congress from a district other than his own. Edward Carrington to Madison, November 19, 1788, and Alexander White to Madison, December 4, 1788, in James Madison Papers, Library of Congress.

20. Albert J. Beveridge, *The Life of John Marshall* (Boston and New York, 1916-19), I, 164-65, 202.

21. It was said that Harrison planned to stand for Norfolk borough, had he failed in Surry. Worthington C. Ford, ed., *Letters of Joseph Jones of Virginia, 1777-1787* (Washington, 1889), 145. See also the sketches of Harrison and Tyler in *Dictionary of American Biography*.

In this connection it may be well to recur to the attempt of the burgesses in 1762 to reduce the minimum freehold requirement of unoccupied land from 100 acres to 50 acres; a proposal which was not approved by the Crown and which was not accomplished until 1785. This attempt has usually been interpreted as a liberal move designed to broaden the voting base. It may just as well, and perhaps more correctly, be viewed as an attempt to multiply the votes of men of property. The poor man was less likely to qualify with unoccupied land than by twenty-five acres with a house on it; and the burgesses made no attempt to reduce this qualification in 1762.

22. J. H. B., *1770-1772*, p. 252.

23. An example of the improper use of this power is reported in *ibid., 1752-1758*, pp. 446-47. Whether the sheriff should prohibit unqualified men from voting or whether he should accept all votes, leaving to the House of Burgesses the purging of polls on complaint of dissatisfied candidates, remained unsettled for many years. For one of many bits of evidence on this moot point see "Virginia Legislature," in *Richmond Enquirer*, February 14, 1822.

24. J. H. B., *1766-1769*, pp. 290-91. The election was conducted by William Eustace, Marshall's successor as sheriff.

25. *Ibid., 1761-1765*, p. 271.

26. Washington, *Diaries*, I, 301 (1768 election); II, 43 (1771 election).

27. Freeman, *Washington*, II, 321 (1758 election); III, 62 (1761 election).

28. Colonel Richard Bland to Theoderick Bland, Sr., February 20, 1745, in Campbell, ed., *Bland Papers*, I, 3-4.

29. Henry St. George Tucker to St. George Tucker, April 4, 1815. Tucker-Coleman Papers.

30. For examples see Buckingham County election of April 14, 1788; Essex County election of April 21, 1788; Spotsylvania County election of April 6(?), 1823; Westmoreland County elections of April 28, 1800; April 25, 1825; and October 25, 1830. Film or photostatic copies of the poll sheets of these elections and those mentioned in the next note are in Virginia State Library.

31. For suggestions in this direction, see Essex County, Deeds No. 41, 1824-[1826], pp. 378-81, election of April 18, 1825; and Westmoreland County, Records & Inventories, No. 2, 1748-1752, election of January 20, 1752.

32. See below, Chapter VII.

33. The vote stood: Thornton, 304, Ball, 255, and Clarke, 97. Poll sheets in Northumberland County, Record Book, 1756-1758, pp. 283-87. Photostatic copy in Virginia State Library. Two volumes, not distinguished by number or otherwise, bear the same title.

34. Poll to elect two burgesses, July 16, 1765, Northumberland County, Record Book, 1762-1766, pt. 2, pp. 643-46. Photostatic copy in Virginia State Library.

	Votes by justices	Total votes
Captain Spencer Mottrom Ball, a justice	15	338
Captain Thomas Gaskins, a justice	14	227
John Cralle, Jr., not a justice	0	159

35. Northumberland County, Record Book, 1770-1772, pp. 271-73. Photostatic copy in Virginia State Library.

36. *Executive Journals of the Council of Colonial Virginia*, V, 391; *Justices of the Peace of Colonial Virginia*, 80-81.

CHAPTER VI

County Oligarchies

1. Malone, *Jefferson*, I, 8.

2. *Ibid.*, 10, 12, 18, 26; *Virginia Magazine of History*, 4 (1896-97),

324. Field Jefferson, uncle of Thomas, was also a justice of the peace. Malone, *Jefferson*, I, 10.

3. *Dictionary of American Biography.*

4. Irving Brant, *James Madison, the Virginia Revolutionist* (Indianapolis, 1941), 307.

5. *Dictionary of American Biography.*

6. Freeman, *Washington*, I, 34, 41.

7. *Ibid.*, I, 229; Hill, *Mason*, 37, 40.

8. Beveridge, *John Marshall*, I, 51-52.

9. Cresson, *Monroe*, 7.

10. *The Candidates*, 36.

11. The sources chiefly relied upon for this discussion of the justices of the peace and the county courts are described in Bibliographical Note: County Court.

12. *Calendar of Virginia State Papers*, IV, 16-17, presents a protest of the Fairfax County Court, dated March 22, 1785, dealing with a current issue but referring to colonial practices. George Mason was present at this meeting of the court.

13. Essex County, Orders, 1773-1782, pt. II, p. 311, photostat in Virginia State Library. A similar recommendation from Augusta County, October 25, 1770, is in *Calendar of Virginia State Papers*, I, 264. Here and subsequently, illustrations of political practices are taken from the early national period as well as from the colonial in those matters, of which there were many, that were unchanged by the American Revolution.

14. *Calendar of Virginia State Papers*, I, 237-38.

15. Tucker, *Blackstone*, bk. I, pt. 1, Appendix, pp. 115-16, 118; *Calendar of Virginia State Papers*, I, 88 (Middlesex County, 1705).

16. *Calendar of Virginia State Papers*, I, 258 (Brunswick County, 1764, petition signed by more than 60 persons).

17. For examples and comments see *Calendar of Virginia State Papers*, I, 98-99, 264; Virginia Constitution of 1776, in Poore, *Federal and State Constitutions*, II, 1911-12; Tucker, *Blackstone*, bk. I, pt. 1, Appendix, pp. 115-16, 118; Essex County, Orders, 1773-1782, pt. II, pp. 310-11. Photostatic copy in Virginia State Library.

18. Essex County, Orders, 1773-1782, pt. II, p. 210. Photostatic copy in Virginia State Library.

19. *Calendar of Virginia State Papers*, I, 264, compared with *Justices of the Peace of Colonial Virginia*, 107.

20. *Calendar of Virginia State Papers*, I, 264.

21. Compare, for example, the recommendations in *Calendar of Virginia State Papers*, I, 264, with the lists of justices in the respective counties in *Justices of the Peace in Colonial Virginia*.

22. *Executive Journals of the Council of Colonial Virginia*, V, 389-95.

23. Calculated from manuscript Commission Book No. 1, in Virginia State Library.

24. A convenient tabulation of the court days of the counties in the year 1790 is on a folded sheet near the end of Jefferson, *Notes on Virginia*. An earlier schedule of court days is in John Mercer, *An Exact Abridgment of All the Public Acts of Assembly of Virginia* (Williamsburg, 1737), 21.

25. *Virginia Gazette* (Purdie and Dixon), November 12, 1767.

26. [Benjamin W. Leigh, comp.,] *The Revised Code of the Laws of Virginia* (Richmond, 1819), I, 244n. Three years earlier Jefferson wrote that to these courts were entrusted "the justice, the executive administration, the taxation, police, the military appointments of the county, and nearly all our daily concerns." Jefferson to John Taylor, May 28, 1816, in Ford, ed., *Writings of Thomas Jefferson*, X, 29.

27. A photostatic copy of the Albemarle County Order Book for this period is in the Virginia State Library. The copies of the records of a large number of Virginia counties in this depository afford an opportunity for making a broad sweep over the activities of the county courts. An excellent summary of the work of the Fairfax County Court, chiefly in the 1760's, is in Hill, *Mason*, 47-56, 268-71.

28. Frederick Johnston, comp., *Memorials of Old Virginia Clerks* ... (Lynchburg, 1888), 23, 26-27, makes the error of assuming that the two Nicholases, father and son, were one person.

29. The overseers of the poor succeeded the vestry in performing the function indicated by their name.

30. Hill, *Mason*, 58n.

31. For an example, Wicomico Parish, Northumberland County, Vestry Book, 1703-1795 (photostat in Virginia State Library), folio 68, vestry meeting of November 10, 1757.

32. Meade, *Old Churches, Ministers and Families of Virginia*, I, 148-51; William Perry, ed., *Historical Collections Relating to the American Colonial Church* ([Hartford], 1870), I, 487.

33. Hill, *Mason*, 58n.

34. Wicomico Parish Vestry Book, 1703-1795, folio 66, compared with the Northumberland County list of justices dated June 7, 1757, in *Justices of the Peace of Colonial Virginia*.

35. South Farnham Parish Vestry Book, 1739-1876 (photostat in Virginia State Library), p. 104, compared with the Essex County list of justices dated June 2, 1774, in *Justices of the Peace of Colonial Virginia.*

36. Meade, *Old Churches, Ministers and Families of Virginia,* I, 151, 153n.

37. Hill, *Mason,* 37-42. The trustee form of town government was customary in colonial Virginia; only in Williamsburg and Norfolk did the inhabitants choose town officials by popular election. Chandler, *History of Suffrage in Virginia,* 14-15, 17-20.

38. These generalizations are based chiefly on a study of the eight counties listed on p. 66.

CHAPTER VII
The House of Burgesses

1. Jefferson, *Notes on Virginia,* 128.

2. Tucker, *Blackstone,* bk. I, pt. 1, Appendix, p. 119. See also p. 81.

3. Section 5 of the Declaration of Rights of the Constitution of 1776. Poore, *Federal and State Constitutions,* II, 1909.

4. Constitution of 1776, in Poore, *Federal and State Constitutions,* II, 1911.

5. John Randolph does not seem to have equalled these men in power despite his tenure of the attorney-generalship. Freeman, *Washington,* III, 3-10, gives a good description of the leading men of the House in the late 1750's, and Elmer I. Miller, *The Legislature of the Province of Virginia; Its Internal Development* (New York, 1907), treats legislative procedure in some detail. See also Stanley M. Pargellis, "Procedure of the Virginia House of Burgesses," *William and Mary Quarterly,* 2d ser., 7 (1927), 73-86, 143-57.

6. A minor exception was the brief service of Richard Lee of Westmoreland as chairman of the Committee of Public Claims for a time in 1772, pending the arrival of Archibald Cary, its former and its subsequent chairman.

7. *Justices of the Peace of Colonial Virginia,* 57, 65, 73, 103.

8. Maury, *Memoir of a Huguenot Family,* 418-24; Moses Coit Tyler, *Patrick Henry* (Boston, 1890), 32-49.

9. A dozen years later Henry, after the death of his first wife, married a daughter of Dandridge.

10. *Justices of the Peace of Colonial Virginia*, 57, 65, 73, 103.

11. For the Dandridge-Littlepage case see *J. H. B., 1761-1765*, pp. 205, 232, 235, 269-72.

12. *Ibid.*, 271.

13. *Ibid.*, 272.

14. *Ibid.*, 315, 345.

15. The best account is by John P. Kennedy in *J. H. B., 1766-1769*, pp. x-xxvi.

16. *J. H. B., 1761-1765*, pp. liv-lviii, Malone, *Jefferson*, I, 91-94.

17. Jefferson to William Wirt, August 14, 1814, and August 5, 1815, in Ford, ed., *Writings of Thomas Jefferson*, IX, 469, 473.

18. These quotations are from the sources given in the previous footnote.

19. Jefferson to William Wirt, August 5, 1815, in Ford, ed., *Writings of Thomas Jefferson*, IX, 473.

20. High on the list of western grievances was its underrepresentation in the House of Burgesses. Although each county was allotted two seats, the western counties had a larger white population. Jefferson estimated in the early 1780's that 19,000 "fighting men" in the counties between the sea coast and the falls of the rivers elected as many senators and nearly as many representatives as some 30,000 "fighting men" living between the fall line and the western limits of Virginia. Jefferson, *Notes on Virginia*, 127-28; also, Tucker, *Blackstone*, bk. I, pt. 1, Appendix, 102-4.

21. For the land valuation tax, see Hening, XI, 140-42, law of 1782.

22. For an analysis of the structure of society in Albemarle County in the eighteenth century see Charles W. Watts, "Land Grants and Aristocracy in Albemarle County, 1727-1775," in Albemarle County Historical Society, *Papers*, 8 (1947-48), especially pp. 18-19.

23. Near the close of the Revolution Jefferson wrote of the contrast between Tidewater and Piedmont, but by 1830 the new state constitution recognized a partnership of these two against the Shenandoah Valley and the mountain country to the westward.

24. It is reassuring to discover that several of the generalizations in this chapter have also been reached by Clinton Rossiter in his Richard Bland: The Whig in America, which I have been allowed to read in manuscript.

25. Malone, *Jefferson*, I, 132-33.

26. Although the electoral college system of choosing presidents of the United States may seem to be an anomaly in the twentieth century, it must have seemed perfectly natural to those eighteenth-century Virginians who had a part in writing it into the Constitution.

27. Constitution of 1776, in Poore, *Federal and State Constitutions*, II, 1910-11; Tucker, *Blackstone*, bk. I, pt. 1, Appendix, p. 113.

CHAPTER VIII
The Pathway to Power

1. The latter statement is based on a sample check of the legislatures of 1776 and 1789. The lists used in this comparison are described in Bibliographical Note: Lists of County, Colonial, and State Officials.
2. Diary of Francis Taylor of Orange County, vol. III, entry for March 24, 1788.
3. Jefferson to William Wirt, August 5, 1815, in Ford, ed., *Writings of Thomas Jefferson*, IX, 474.
4. Instances in which burgesses voted contrary to the known wishes of their constituents are given in Hubbell and Adair's Introduction to Robert Munford, *The Candidates*, 10.
5. *Pennsylvania Evening Post*, April 27, 1776, quoted in Frank Moore, ed., *Diary of the American Revolution, from Newspapers and Original Documents* (New York, 1860), I, 237-38.
6. The *Journals of the House of Burgesses* mention innumerable petitions. See also H. J. Eckenrode, ed., *A Calendar of Legislative Petitions Arranged by Counties, Accomac—Bedford* (Richmond, 1908), and Charles F. James, comp., *Documentary History of the Struggle for Religious Liberty in Virginia* (Lynchburg, 1900).

CHAPTER IX
The Eighteenth Century to the Twentieth

1. In South Carolina, to the contrary, a man was sometimes elected when he was absent and when he apparently did not know that he was being considered. Having been so elected, the South Carolinian sometimes refused to serve. For examples, see Charleston *South-Carolina Gazette*, October 18-26, 1760; March 28-April 4, 1761.
2. See for example the important act of 1736 in Hening, IV, 475-78.
3. John Taliaferro to Chairman of the Committee of Elections, in papers of the disputed election case of John Taliaferro vs. John P. Hungerford, 12th Congress (1811), in the files of the House of Representatives, in National Archives.

4. Charles S. Sydnor, *The Development of Southern Sectionalism, 1819-1848* ([Baton Rouge,] 1948), 43-49, 215-20.

5. Jefferson to J. C. Cabell, January 24, 1816, in Francis N. Cabell, *Early History of the University of Virginia as Contained in the Letters of Thomas Jefferson and Joseph C. Cabell* (Richmond, 1856), 48.

6. Jefferson to John Tyler, May 28, 1816, in Ford, ed., *Writings of Thomas Jefferson*, X, 29-30.

7. Jefferson to John Adams, October 28, 1813, in *ibid.*, IX, 427; "Revisal of the Laws, 1776-1786," in Boyd, Butterfield, and Bryan, eds., *Papers of Thomas Jefferson*, II, 391-93.

8. Jefferson, *Notes on Virginia*, 157.

9. Jefferson, "Report of the Commissioners Appointed to Fix the Site of the University of Virginia," in Cabell, ed., *Early History of the University of Virginia*, 437.

10. Jefferson to John Adams, October 28, 1813, in Ford, ed., *Writings of Thomas Jefferson*, IX, 427.

11. Munford, *The Candidates*, 38.

12. Malone, *Jefferson*, I, 394.

13. Among the few studies that trace the lessening of aristocratic forces in American government are Dixon Ryan Fox, *The Decline of Aristocracy in the Politics of New York* (New York, 1919), and Walter R. Fee, *The Transition from Aristocracy to Democracy in New Jersey, 1789-1829* (Somerville, N. J., 1933).

Index

Accomac County, 54; election quarrel in, 46

Albemarle County, 28, 31, 66, 92, 139, 142, 163

Albemarle County Court, summary of activities, 86-90

Alderson, Reverend John, 28

Alexandria, 25, 58, 79, 92

Ambler, Jacquelin, 79

Ambler, Mary Willis, 79

Amelia County, 138

Amherst County, compulsory voting an issue in, 33

Aristocracy, as a balance to democracy, 119, 125-26, 132-34; Jefferson's distrust of hereditary, 127-30; his plan for discovering and training the "natural" aristocracy, 128-30. *See* Gentlemen of eighteenth-century Virginia

Assembly, supremacy over executive branch of government, 95-96; electoral powers of, 95-96. *See* House of Burgesses

Attorney general of Virginia, 96-97

Augusta County, riotous election in, 15-19

Ball, Spencer Mottrom, 19, 83, 165

Baptists, 117; voting by, 28

Ben, a slave, 87

Bernard, Captain Robert, improper electioneering by, 54-55

Beverley, Robert, 81

Blackwell, John, 88

Bland, Richard, 74, 97-105, 108, 115

Bland, Theoderick, Jr., quoted, 51

Bland, Theoderick, Sr., 74

Boswell, John, 44

Botetourt, Governor, 107

Botetourt County, 84

Bradley, Eliza, 35

Brodie, Doctor John, 23

Buckingham County, 31, 75, 138, 142

Bullivant, James, Jr., 36

Bullivant, Philip, 35

Burgesses, lists of, 149. *See* Candidates for office; House of Burgesses

Burwell, Lewis, 63, 99

Bushrod, John, 21

Byrd, Mary, 163

Campaign practices, 41-59, 72-73, 102-3. *See* Candidates for office

Candidates for office, dealings with each other, 40-41, 46; dealings with voters, 27-28, 41-59, 102-3;

INDEX

Vestry, powers of, 90-92; autonomous, 91; and county court, 91

Virginia, University of, 7

Viva Voce voting. *See* Oral voting

Voters, qualifications of, 28-29; freehold requirements of, 29-31, 37, 164; reasons for freehold requirements of, 122-23; disqualified, how dealt with, 20-21; number entitled to vote, 31-32; percentage who voted, 32, 38; compulsory voting, 32-33; plural voting, 70, 72; general description of, 37-38; class divisions among, 69, 75-76; simplicity of their task, 123-24; statistics on, 142-43

"Vulgar Herd, The," chapter title, 27; quotation, 61

Wager, William, 22, 48, 52-53; treating the voters, 57-58

Wallace, James, 22

Waring, Thomas, 81

Washington, George, 1, 91, 99, 107, 111-12, 115; prominence of family, 79; first election as burgess,

68-70; later elections, 19, 20, 25; campaign expenses of, 19, 51, 73; treating the voters, 53-54, 58; fight on election day, 24-25; political advice to, 41

Washington, Lawrence, 79

West, Hugh, 68-69, 76

West, John, 24, 75

Westmoreland County, 21, 75, 138

Whiting, Beverley, 54-55

Whiting, Thomas, 99

Wicomico Parish, 91

William and Mary, College of, 3; burgess of, 14, 34

Williamsburg, 34; burgess of, 14; its citizens oppose treating by candidates, 55-56

Winchester, 41. *See* Frederick County

Woddrop, William, 81

Wood, James, 68-70

Woods, Richard, principal in a riotous election, 16-18

Wythe, George, 79, 108, 110, 112; as burgess, 34; campaign strategy of, 48; power in House of Burgesses, 97-99, 103, 105